Bare Ruined Choirs

Bare Ruined Choirs

Sacred Spaces In Four Early Modern Plays

Lisa Hopkins

ANTHEM PRESS

Anthem Press
An imprint of Wimbledon Publishing Company
www.anthempress.com

This edition first published in UK and USA 2025
by ANTHEM PRESS
75–76 Blackfriars Road, London SE1 8HA, UK
or PO Box 9779, London SW19 7ZG, UK
and
244 Madison Ave #116, New York, NY 10016, USA

© 2025 Lisa Hopkins

The author asserts the moral right to be identified as the author of this work.

All rights reserved. Without limiting the rights under copyright reserved above, no part of this publication may be reproduced, stored or introduced into a retrieval system, or transmitted, in any form or by any means (electronic, mechanical, photocopying, recording or otherwise), without the prior written permission of both the copyright owner and the above publisher of this book.

British Library Cataloguing-in-Publication Data
A catalogue record for this book is available from the British Library.

Library of Congress Cataloging-in-Publication Data: 2025931693
A catalog record for this book has been requested.

ISBN-13: 978-1-83999-511-8 (Pbk)
ISBN-10: 1-83999-511-4 (Pbk)

This title is also available as an e-book.

CONTENTS

Acknowledgements		vii
Introduction		ix
1.	Thorney Abbey	1
2.	A Knack to Know a Knave	15
3.	A Shoemaker a Gentleman	27
4.	The Lovesick King	39
Coda		49
Index		51

ACKNOWLEDGEMENTS

With thanks to Bill Angus, Matt Steggle, Rob Crichton and the Beyond Shakespeare team from whose reading of *A Knack to Know a Knave* (available on YouTube) I learned a great deal, and the anonymous reader for the press, who made two perfectly obvious points which I had totally failed to see for myself. Thanks as always to Chris and Sam; if we hadn't had to divert to the Jewel Tower that day I would never have thought of this book.

INTRODUCTION

In the opening scene of Shakespeare's *Henry V*, the Archbishop of Canterbury complains to the Bishop of Ely that there are plans afoot to divest the church of some of the property which has been bequeathed to it in the wills of lay people: 'all the temporal lands which men devout / By testament have given to the Church / Would they strip from us'.[1] Stuart Elden explains that

> 'temporal lands' [...] are lands that the church owns directly as landlord, not by nature of their spiritual power but because of their earthly wealth. The struggle between church and king over such lands recurs through European history of this period. Shakespeare had explored it before. It was a significant theme in *King John*, for example, with the Bastard sent to raid the monasteries at the same time that the King is in dispute with Pope Innocent III and his legate, Cardinal Pandulph, over jurisdiction in the English kingdom.[2]

The tension between spiritual and temporal overlordship of lands is also present in other early modern plays. Scenes in which lay persons seeking justice are stopped on the threshold of spiritual spaces occur in Ford's *Tis Pity She's a Whore* and in Shakespeare's *The Comedy of Errors*, while in Webster's *The Duchess of Malfi*, the Duchess is taken by surprise when a trip to Loreto brings her into the power of her brother the Cardinal; the uneasy relationship between temporal and spiritual is troubled still further here by the fact that the Cardinal has donned armour. More subtly, in Middleton's *The Lady's Tragedy* the Tyrant commands one of his followers 'Bring me the keys of the Cathedral straight' (4.2.39), but First Soldier is unhappy about the idea of robbing a church because he believes that 'What's got from grace, is ever spent in law' (4.2.57)[3]; the Tyrant may feel he has the right to enter the cathedral, but ironically First Soldier thinks that whether or not there is a divine or an ecclesiastical response to his sacrilege, the secular power of the courts will certainly be brought to bear in a case involving church property. First Soldier posits both an opposition and a collusion of sorts between 'grace' and 'law' which will marginalise and disadvantage the titular head of state.

In the anonymous domestic tragedy *Arden of Faversham*, which I touch on in Chapter 3, the Kent town of Faversham can be seen as invisibly but potently divided into zones. The creek and its quay are the town's gateway to the world outside, and the source of much of its prosperity; the guildhall and Queen Elizabeth's Grammar School stand for civic authority and the skills needed to thrive in secular society; but the Ardens' back garden was once the property of Faversham Abbey and seems to retain some element of sacred status when the snow which falls there quasi-miraculously reveals the truth about Arden's murder. Thomas Rist terms the play a 'sacrilege narrative', that is one which 'show[s] the destruction of persons or families who took monastic land at the Dissolution of the Monasteries, implying they are providentially punished for theft of sacred land',[4] and in this book, I aim to build on that concept as I explore some of the ways in which sacred and secular spheres of influence could come into conflict as represented in four plays from the late sixteenth and early seventeenth centuries. I am interested in the extent to which those spheres of influence map onto actual territory, but also in the ways in which land is perceived as retaining memories of uses to which it has been previously put. This was particularly the case when royal or saintly bodies had been buried in it, even if the actual burials had been disturbed or lost completely, but other kinds of spaces and places could also carry with them a sense of an ineradicable past (often a specifically pre-Reformation past). When plays claim to represent such richly suggestive sites as holy wells, abbeys built before the Norman Conquest, or places where martyrdoms or miracles have occurred, they simultaneously suggest the power and appeal of such memories and yet also acknowledge their loss and inaccessibility, not least because what the audience sees is *not* the place represented but bare boards of the stage standing in for it.

As this brief survey suggests, there are a lot of plays which I could have used to talk about the demarcation of secular and sacred territory, but the four plays I have chosen to focus on are the anonymous *Thorney Abbey* and *A Knack to Know a Knave*, William Rowley's *A Shoemaker a Gentleman*, and Anthony Brewer's *The Lovesick King*. I have picked these firstly because of the sites they present or refer to: in *Thorney Abbey*, the original foundation which later became Westminster Abbey, discussed in terms which remind us that both the modern abbey and the Houses of Parliament are built on land which was once visibly an island; in *A Knack to Know a Knave* the northern English town of Hexham, whose status had recently undergone a legal change and where a famous battle had been fought; in *A Shoemaker a Gentleman*, the heady coupling of the important North Welsh pilgrimage site of St Winifred's Well and St Albans, the place where England's first martyr died; and in *The Lovesick King*, a trajectory from a royal necropolis at Winchester to Newcastle, characterised as home to both incomparably strong city walls and also a church which memorialises local achievement.

My second reason for this selection is that each of these plays is in one way or another in dialogue either with Shakespeare or (in the case of *A Knack to Know a Knave*) Marlowe. Both Shakespeare and Marlowe are now understood as national playwrights who use the genre of the history play to talk to us about English identities in ways we still consider relevant today: if the UK fights a war someone stages *Henry V*, and when Margaret Thatcher's government tried to define British culture as exclusively heteronormative Derek Jarman made a film of *Edward II*. But both are also *local* writers, interested not just in England in general but in towns and cities ranging from Dover and Southampton to Scarborough and York, and by the same token the fact that my four chosen plays talk about specific localities does not preclude them from participating in wider national debates about memory, identity and the nature of sacredness. I am not suggesting that *Thorney Abbey* could ever fill the National Theatre in the way that *Hamlet* can, but I do propose that it is participating in the same sort of debates about the impact of the Reformation and the importance of bodily remains, and reading these lesser-known plays against more famous ones sheds light in both directions.

Since the dates of the plays themselves are uncertain I have treated them roughly in regnal order, as far as this can be guessed – so starting with Edmund (and perhaps his predecessor Athelstan), moving on to Edgar, plumping for somewhere in the middle of the unholy trinity of Alfred the Great, Eadred and Offa who all apparently co-exist in *A Shoemaker a Gentleman*, and ending with the tenth-century Canute. However, I also consider the plays both in relation to each other and to their Shakespeare or Marlowe 'pair'. The preferred Shakespeare text is usually *Hamlet*, *Macbeth* or *Henry V*, but *A Shoemaker a Gentleman* has strong echoes of *Cymbeline* as well as of *Henry V* because, in both *Cymbeline* and *A Shoemaker a Gentleman*, there is an episode set in Wales in which an attempted rape by a loathed suitor is thwarted by a wronged and virtuous woman and in both plays, someone thought to have been beheaded subsequently comes back to life (St Winifred herself, Posthumus). One might even be tempted to compare Winifred's subsequent marriage to Christ as a nun with Imogen's marriage to Posthumus, which is explicitly spiritualised by Posthumus when he says, 'Hang there like fruit, my soul, / Till the tree die'.[5]

There are reasons why these four Shakespeare plays should be so strongly remembered in my chosen texts, because they all reflect on unquiet burials, and the plays I discuss here all focus on or feature the foundation or embellishment of significant ecclesiastical sites, most of which had been damaged or destroyed during the Dissolution of the Monasteries. These range from the relatively insignificant All Hallows Church in Newcastle to the royal necropolis at Westminster Abbey, and also include St Albans Cathedral, St Winifred's Well in Wales, Hexham Abbey, Faversham Abbey and Winchester Cathedral. It is impossible to overestimate the difference such buildings made to England at the time of their foundation: Max Adams notes that the first stone structure built after the departure of the Romans was York Minister and Hexham Abbey the second,[6] while another great religious centre, Lindisfarne, brought literacy to the area. It is also difficult to overstate the social and ideological disruption caused by the Reformation, which disrupted even where it did not dissolve ecclesiastical foundations and laid bare tensions between secular and sacred.

Most of the plays I discuss are interested not just in religious houses but in royal burials, particularly those of pre-Conquest kings; the exception to this rule is *A Knack to Know a Knave*, but I have suggested that its silence on this subject is a loud one. As several scholars have noted, there was intense and highly politicised interest in the Anglo-Saxons during the sixteenth and seventeenth centuries. Glyn Parry and Cathryn Enis note the particular intensity which surrounded the ancestry of the important Warwickshire family of Arden, with which Shakespeare may have believed himself connected on his mother's side: 'The Ardens descended from Turchil, a leading Saxon magnate in the Midlands and lord of Warwick at the Norman Conquest', making the head of the family, Edward Arden, 'the one man in Warwickshire with a documented pre-Conquest past', but this was a source of irritation to Ambrose Dudley, Earl of Warwick, and his brother Robert, Earl of Leicester and favourite of Queen Elizabeth: 'By the 1570s, the Dudleys were attempting to connect the Beauchamp patrimony of the earldom of Warwick with the pre-Conquest estates attributed to such legendary figures as Guy of Warwick and Sayerus Sutton, mythical ancestor of the Lords Dudley of Sutton, via real figures such as Turchil', with the result that 'this lineage dispute brought the legend of Guy of Warwick and the history of Saxon England to the forefront of public discourse'.[7] More generally, Donna Hamilton observes that 'Over the sixty-year period from 1565 to 1625, the discourse of Catholic Saxonism was generated primarily in regard to three related topics: the origins of Christianity in England, the opposition between papal and royal supremacy, and the succession question, first, in regard to the succession to Elizabeth and, next, in regard to the impending succession and marriage of Prince Charles'. She argues that 'Catholics used precedents from Anglo-Saxon history not only to argue that to be Christian was to be Catholic, but to urge their point that to be English was to be Catholic' and shows that the Catholic Thomas Stapleton's translation of Bede prompted John Foxe to revise *Acts and Monuments* to mention, amongst other Anglo-Saxons whom he had not previously discussed, Alfred, Athelstan, Edmund,

Edgar and Dunstan, although he uses them to argue against Catholic practice and papal authority rather than for them.[8] (John Guy and Julia Fox observe that according to the martyrologist John Foxe, Henry would 'merely be "restoring" to himself legitimate royal rights which, historically, Anglo-Saxon and Norman kings had exercised, and which the papacy had usurped'.)[9] As for the stage, Lawrence Manley and Sally Beth Maclean have identified 'Saxon history' as 'a demonstrable interest of Strange's Men'.[10]

Recorded burials of Anglo-Saxon saints and kings (which could be overlapping categories) were of particular interest. Thomas Williams remarks that 'There were few more unequivocal ways of marking territorial claims in the early Middle Ages than by planting royal corpses in the soil',[11] while Nicole Marafioti notes that 'royal tombs were coveted by monastic communities' and that 'royal burial was a rich, established, and effective mode of political discourse'; she argues that 'A ruler's corpse was a volatile symbolic object which needed to be carefully defined and controlled during moments of political crisis: just as a king's reign would be framed and interpreted by contemporary chroniclers, his body would be ascribed a particular identity in the days following his death and burial'.[12] (Burying them also, of course, proves that they're dead, forestalling any such troubles as those of Henry V, who was plagued by rumours that Richard II had survived, or Henry VII, who was repeatedly troubled by pretenders.) As a result, the bodies of rulers might subsequently be translated as geopolitical priorities changed: Peter Rex observes that 'Aethelstan moved the body of St Oswald from Barney in Lincolnshire to Gloucester, St Werburg from Hanbury, Staffordshire, to Chester, and St Eahlmund from Derby to Shrewsbury, all as part of the building of strengthening of burhs in those places'.[13] Even a lost royal body could have power, not least because such corpses had a habit of reappearing: King Edward the Martyr's stepmother supposedly concealed his corpse but it was miraculously recovered, and similar stories of loss and retrieval were told of Edmund and Oswald, both of whom were kings as well as saints. St Oswald, subject of the lost *Play of Oswald* and first king of Northumbria, died at Oswestry in the Welsh marches; his skull, initially displayed on a pike there, later became a relic of Durham Cathedral, but Alexandra Walsham notes that 'In Shropshire the tradition that St Oswald's arm had been hung on an old tree "lately standing" in the parish of Oswestry after his death in battle in 642 remained fixed in collective consciousness as late as 1635'.[14]

Nor did the interest in Anglo-Saxon royal bodies disappear after the Conquest: in 1589, in his account of how he travelled with his master Henry Cavendish (son of Bess of Hardwick) to Constantinople, a servant who identifies himself only as 'Fox' noted that in Magdeburg 'ther ys a great churche called the Doome [*Dom*], and ther we wear shewed the toome of

Edethe the Empresse, the wyf of Ottan, Emperour. Thys Edethe was the daughter [actually sister] of Ethellstane, Kyng of Ingland'.[15] As I discuss in the chapter on *Thorney Abbey*, Athelstan was an important figure who was well remembered in Elizabethan and Jacobean England, but there seems to be a more general sense that the tomb of an Anglo-Saxon princess would automatically be of interest to visiting Englishmen.

Hamlet, *Macbeth*, *Henry V* and *Cymbeline* are all directly interested in royal burials. In *Hamlet*, a royal grave cannot contain a ghost and the play may also just possibly remember St Olaf, King of Norway, to whom both the parish church of Elsinore and Shakespeare's own local church when he was living in Silver Street were dedicated,[16] as well as a church close to the Globe in Southwark. In *Macbeth*, sacred power resides in a stone, while *Henry V* might have reminded audiences of the body of Catherine of Valois, left unburied and still on open display at Westminster Abbey at the time when the play was written.[17] Both *Henry V* and the *Henry VI* plays are also concerned with the question of how holy is too holy: Henry VI is too saint-like to be kingly, but Henry V is anxious not only to defend church property – Bardolph is hanged for robbing a church – but also to parlay piety into worldly success, hoping that the chantries he has built for the soul of Richard II (after having his body translated from its original burial place of King's Langley to Westminster Abbey) will count in his favour on the battlefield.

Cymbeline is if anything even more deeply invested in old royal funerary rites. During the course of the play, we see the funerals of both the stepson and the daughter of a pre-Conquest king, and both are deeply problematic: Cloten, Cymbeline's stepson, is beheaded and his body thrown into a stream, and Innogen's funeral becomes the subject of heated debate (leaving aside for the moment the fact that she is not actually dead) when Guiderius says 'Nay, Cadwal, we must lay his head to th'east. / My father hath a reason for't' (4.2.254–5). As I have discussed elsewhere,[18] both which way the head should lie, and whether it *mattered* which way the head should lie, were topics of hot debate. Margaret Jones-Davies notes that 'Roman Catholics would usually insist on being buried with their heads to the west so that they would face the east at the Judgement Day' but that 'the direction of the bodies was dismissed as superstition by the reformers',[19] and Eamon Duffy confirms that 'The Admonition to Parliament of 1572 complained of the superstitions used "bothe in Countrye and Citie, for the place of buriall, which way they muste lie"'.[20] Paul Hyland observes that

> When Sir Walter Ralegh laid his head on the executioner's block in Palace Yard in 1618 he knelt facing the wrong way. He looked west towards Devon, where he was born sixty-five years earlier, and in the

direction of a New World which had seduced and undone him. The
Dean of Westminster pointed out his error. A man about to cross the
threshold of eternity must lie with his face towards the east, the promised
land and the resurrected Christ.[21]

Guiderius apparently concurs with the Dean of Westminster but seems not
to know the reason for it, suggesting a society clinging to practices it has
inherited from its elders but no longer understands. In fact, Innogen is not
actually buried at all: if she had been, she could not simply get up and walk
away with Caius Lucius, nor would he have seen her in the first place.

Cymbeline is Shakespeare's name for Cunobelinus, a historical king of the
Catuvellauni. He is one of several kings to feature in my chosen plays. *Thorney
Abbey* has a king who is never identified (though I suggest that we might think
of Athelstan) succeeded by his brother Edmund, a resonant and important
name whose implications I discuss and I argue that the play also evokes the
rivalry between Hardicanute and his putative half-brother Harold Harefoot.
A Knack to Know a Knave features King Edgar; *The Lovesick King* has Alfred the
Great anachronistically fighting Canute and *A Shoemaker a Gentleman* plays
even more fast and loose with history by having Alfred the Great father two
sons named Offa and Eldred.

As well as kings, there is considerable interest in saints in the four plays on
which I focus. Particularly important is St Dunstan, who refounded Westminster
Abbey[22] and encouraged King Edgar in his programme of reintroducing
Benedictine monasticism to England; he is a central figure in *A Knack to Know a
Knave*, and St Winifred, St Alban, St Amphibalus, St Hugh and SS Crispin and
Crispian also feature in the plays I discuss. My central argument is that these
plays are engaged in a coded way of lamenting the Dissolution of the Monasteries,
reflecting Alexandra Walsham's identification of 'the sense of loss' felt by many
after the Dissolution of the Monasteries.[23] Individually and collectively, these
four plays also put pressure on memories of that loss in Shakespeare, whose
evocative phrase 'bare ruined choirs' has indeed supplied my title. Alison A.
Chapman notes that Ophelia's 'descent into grief and madness is marked by
a surge of allusions to medieval Catholic forms of piety St. James, St. Charity,
"old lauds", pilgrimage to the shrine of Our Lady of Walsingham, and other
pre-Reformation religious folklore' in a way that 'calls attention to the loss of
the Walsingham shrine itself',[24] originally founded in the tenth century, while
Stewart Mottram observes that '*Cymbeline* contains several references to wrecks
and ruins'.[25] These might seem like minor elements of their respective texts, but
understanding the ways in which Shakespeare is in dialogue with other plays
more openly about loss can help us see how poignant and resonant such small
moments could have been on stage.

All these plays implicitly propose that power inheres in place; however, they not only stage what Pierre Nora has called 'Lieux de Mémoire' but specifically suggest that anywhere which has once been sanctified by the inhumation of a royal or saintly body retains sacred status even if buildings have been destroyed and communities dispersed. This was in itself a controversial position. Alexandra Walsham notes that 'In his *Survey of Popery* of 1596, Thomas Bell was [...] scathing about "the sinister and false perswasion" that "gadding to visit stocks, stones, and dead mens bones" could help to secure one's salvation', while 'Preaching in Fife before 1534, William Arth firmly repudiated the notion that the Virgin Mary "took more pleasour in one place then in ane uther" and capriciously transferred her patronage of particular locations, "as of laite dayis our Lady of Karsgreng hes hopped fra ane grene hillock to ane uther"'. The market cross in Cheapside was a particular flashpoint: contemporaries noted that 'Edmund Campion had bowed to it on his way to Tyburn in 1581, while in 1595 William Freeman "did reverence thereunto" by removing his hat'. Nevertheless, Walsham observes that 'There is plentiful evidence that people of all social ranks continued to frequent hallowed places that had been vandalized or abandoned in the course of the Long Reformation'.[26] Such journeys are what these plays imaginatively perform, while simultaneously conceding that they cannot do so physically.

Each play also contains a crossover figure who inhabits both the spiritual and the secular realms. Edgar in *A Knack to Know a Knave* rules the kingdom and also founds monasteries; Amphiabel in *A Shoemaker a Gentleman* is a 'seminary knight', so simultaneously priest and warrior; Old Thorney in *Thorney Abbey* starts his life as a burgess and ends it in the abbey he has founded; and Roger Thornton in *The Lovesick King* simultaneously builds city walls and embellishes a church. To think of it in another way, each of these figures is identifiable with both an earthly lodging and a grave or tomb, particularly in the case of Amphiabel, who seems to live close to St Winifred's Well but whose shrine in the cathedral of St Albans (under his more usual name of Amphibalus) was second in importance only to that of Alban himself. Philip Schwyzer notes that 'The Reformation, with its deep scepticism regarding relics and prayers for departed souls, radically transformed the spiritual status of human remains. No longer could fragmented bodies serve as the conduits through which spiritual aid flowed between the dead and the living [...] In some cases [...] Protestants seem to have made a self-conscious show of their new-found contempt for human carcasses'; he observes 'The naked aggression displayed towards the medieval dead in the turbulent years of Reformation'.[27] In this respect, the four plays I discuss here come especially close to Shakespeare and also to Marlowe. *Doctor Faustus* references Sant'Angelo, an archetypal crossover location in that it was both the mausoleum of the Emperor Hadrian and the fortress of the Pope, and both it and *Hamlet* ask whether what remains is physical or spiritual or both: Philip Schwyzer suggestively argues that after *Titus Andronicus* and *Romeo and Juliet*, '*Hamlet* is the third of Shakespeare's mortuary tragedies, and the most unflinching in its determination to confront the secrets of the grave',[28] while for Peter McCullough, '*Hamlet* can be seen as a poignant, and therefore nostalgic and conservative, lament for the loss at the Reformation of a world of ecclesiastical and epistemological certainties'.[29] *Hamlet* gives us both a skull and a ghost and leaves us to choose which if either is a truer representation of the person who has gone, while Doctor Faustus conjures up simulacra of the classical dead which mimic their appearance but cannot be touched; dead bodies are at the heart of these plays' ideological projects, and yet the meaning and status of those bodies is radically unclear. That is also the case for *Thorney Abbey*, *A Knack to Know a Knave*, *A Shoemaker a Gentleman* and *The Lovesick King*, which collectively conduct an enquiry into unquiet royal graves and what they say about early modern England.

Notes

1 William Shakespeare, *King Henry V*, edited by T. W. Craik (London: Routledge, 1995), 1.1.9–11.
2 Stuart Elden, *Shakespearean Territories* (Chicago: University of Chicago Press, 2018), pp. 114–5.
3 Julia Briggs, ed., *The Lady's Tragedy: Parallel Texts*, in *Thomas Middleton: The Collected Works*, edited by Gary Taylor and John Lavagnino (Oxford: The Clarendon Press, 2010), pp. 833–906.
4 Thomas Rist, 'Arden of Feversham as "Sacrilege Narrative', *Notes and Queries* 57.3 (2010): 355–6. He takes the phrase from Alison Shell, *Oral Culture and Catholicism in Early Modern England* (Cambridge, 2007), 23–54, though he notes that Shell does not mention *Arden* in her discussion.
5 William Shakespeare, *Cymbeline*, edited by J. M. Nosworthy (London: Cengage Learning, 2007), 5.5.263–4.
6 Max Adams, *The King in the North*, p. 295.
7 Glyn Parry and Cathryn Enis, *Shakespeare before Shakespeare: Stratford-upon-Avon, Warwickshire, and the Elizabethan State* (Oxford: Oxford University Press, 2020), pp. 11–12.
8 Donna Hamilton, 'Catholic Use of Anglo-Saxon Precedents, 1565–1625', *Recusant History* 26.4 (October 2003), pp. 537–55, pp. 537 and 541–2.
9 John Guy and Julia Fox, *Hunting the Falcon* (London: Bloomsbury, 2023), Kindle loc. 3891.
10 Lawrence Manley and Sally Beth Maclean, *Lord Strange's Men and Their Plays* (New Haven: Yale University Press, 2014), p. 151.
11 Thomas Williams, *Lost Realms: Histories of Britain from the Romans to the Vikings* (London: William Collins, 2022), pp. 133–4.
12 Nicole Marafioti, *The King's Body: Burial and Succession in Late Anglo-Saxon England* (Toronto: University of Toronto Press, 2014), pp. 181 and 253 and 5.

13 Peter Rex, *Edgar, King of the English 959–75* (Stroud: Tempus, 2007), p. 164.
14 Alexandra Walsham, *The Reformation of the Landscape: Religion, Identity, and Memory in Early Modern Britain and Ireland* (Oxford: Oxford University Press, 2011), p. 487.
15 A. C. Wood, ed., *Mr Harrie Cavendish his Journey to and from Constantinople 1589 by Fox, his Servant*, Camden Miscellany vol. 17 (London: Royal Historical Society, 1940), p. 22.
16 David Hohnen, *Hamlet's Castle and Shakespeare's Elsinore* (Copenhagen: Christian Ejlers, 2000), p. 22.
17 https://www.westminster-abbey.org/abbey-commemorations/royals/henry-v-and-catherine-de-valois
18 Lisa Hopkins, *From the Romans to the Normans on the English Renaissance Stage* (ARC Humanities Press, 2017), p. 147.
19 Margaret Jones-Davies, '*Cymbeline* and the sleep of faith', in *Theatre and religion: Lancastrian Shakespeare*, edited by Richard Dutton, Alison Findlay, and Richard Wilson (Manchester: Manchester University Press, 2003), pp. 197–217, p. 211.
20 Eamon Duffy, *The Stripping of the Altars: Traditional Religion in England, c. 1400–c. 1580* (New Haven: Yale University Press, 1992), p. 578.
21 Paul Hyland, *Ralegh's Last Journey* (London: HarperCollins, 2003), p. 1.
22 Marafioti, *The King's Body*, p. 243.
23 Alexandra Walsham, *The Reformation of the Landscape: Religion, Identity, and Memory in Early Modern Britain and Ireland* (Oxford: Oxford University Press, 2011), 274.
24 Alison A. Chapman, 'Ophelia's "Old Lauds": Madness and Hagiography in *Hamlet*', *Medieval & Renaissance Drama in England* 20 (2007), pp. 111–135, pp. 111 and 127.
25 Stewart Mottram, 'Warriors and Ruins: *Cymbeline*, Heroism and the Union of Crowns', in *Celtic Shakespeare: The Bard and the Borderers*, edited by Willy Maley and Rory Loughnane (Farnham: Ashgate, 2013), pp. 168–183, p. 174.
26 Walsham, *The Reformation of the Landscape*, pp. 83, 99, 233, and 166.
27 Philip Schwyzer, *Archaeologies of English Renaissance Literature* (Oxford: Oxford University Press, 2007), pp. 110–11.
28 Schwyzer, *Archaeologies of English Renaissance Literature*, p. 133.
29 Peter McCullough, 'Christmas at Elsinore', *Essays in Criticism* 58.4 (2008): 311–332, 311–12.

Chapter 1

THORNEY ABBEY

I want to start by focusing on a play which is ostensibly free of tensions between the spiritual and temporal but which in fact offers subtle hints of the problematic conceptual boundary between sacred and secular. Nicole Marafioti notes that at some point during the reign of William the Conqueror 'the monk Sulcard was commissioned to write an account of Westminster [Abbey]'s construction'.[1] Echoes of that history can be found in an anonymous play called *Thorney Abbey*, which offers an origin story for the Anglo-Saxon foundation which preceded the Norman Westminster Abbey (and stood on the same site, so is not to be confused with the Thorney Abbey near Peterborough). *Thorny-Abbey*, or *The London-Maid; a Tragedy*, by T.W. was first printed in 1662 in *Gratiae Theatrales, or A choice Ternary of English Plays, Composed upon especial occasions by several ingenious persons*, the other members of the 'ternary' being *The Marriage-Broker* or *The Pander; a Comedy*, by M. W. M. A. and *Grim the Collier of Croydon, or The Devil and his Dame; with the Devil and St. Dunstan: a Comedy*, by I. T.[2] Despite the title page's attribution to 'T. W.' Lucy Munro notes that William Rowley and Thomas Heywood have both been suggested as authors and tentatively dates the play c. 1606–16.[3]

Thorney Abbey offers an account of the foundation of the future Westminster Abbey during the reign of an unnamed king of England who has a brother (and heir) called Edmund. This was a suggestive name. Francis Young's book *Edmund: In Search of England's Lost King* notes the extraordinary importance and continuing resonance of the story of the Anglo-Saxon St Edmund, who 'became a shorthand with which kings could summon up, in one image, an idea of old-fashioned English monarchy': 'St Edmund's royal symbolism remained potent enough for a tiny figure of the saint to be included in Henry VIII's crown'; he features in *Acts and Monuments*; and he was mentioned by Drayton and Laurence Nowell. He was particularly important to English Catholic exiles: there were images of him in the English Colleges at Rome and Seville because 'Edmund embodied an ideal form of Catholic kingship' and was 'the perfect vehicle for the reaffirmation of Catholic Englishness'.[4] Closer to home, St Edmund supports Richard II in the Wilton Diptych and was remembered in the names of two Tudors, the father and youngest son of Henry VII. He was certainly an appropriate figure to mention in a play about Westminster Abbey: Francis Young notes that 'By 1300 a banner of St Edmund was displayed in Westminster Abbey' and that 'The chapel of St Edmund in Westminster Abbey was located next to the chapel of St Edward the Confessor'.[5]

It seems odd, though, that while Edmund is named repeatedly, the king his brother never is. Just possibly, this was because he didn't need to be. Lucy Munro regards *Thorney Abbey* as part of a group of plays:

> Within *Hengist, The Birth of Merlin, The Welsh Ambassador* and *Thorney Abbey*, anachronistic elements or fragments, such as linguistic archaism and neologism, prophecy, and palimpsest, possess the capacity to collapse the boundaries between past and present or to mediate between competing narratives about the past.[6]

I have noted elsewhere that one of these plays, *The Welsh Embassador*, a 1621 collaboration between Thomas Dekker, William Rowley, and John Ford, is one of a number of early modern plays about King Athelstan,[7] though that does not preclude it also having a connection with *Thorney Abbey* (both *The Welsh Embassador* and *Thorney Abbey* are haunted by memories of *Macbeth* and both glance too at the causes and effects of the English Reformation). Athelstan, eldest son of Alfred the Great's son Edward the Elder, was king of England from 925 to 939, but he never married, and there are hints in the Anglo-Saxon Chronicle and his obviously frosty relationship with Winchester, the traditional capital of his ancestors, that his succession to the throne was regarded in some quarters as problematic.[8] Sarah Foot suggests that this was because all of Athelstan's younger brothers 'had been born to a ruling king',[9] but it is more generally taken to be connected to his illegitimacy, with the theory being that he may have deliberately chosen celibacy in recognition of the unmarried status of his mother: thus although he might reign himself he would not act as a transmitter of the royal bloodline, which would revert instead to one of the thirteen legitimate children of his father Edward the Elder (as Robert Persons has it in *A conference about the next succession to the crowne of Ingland*, 'This man dying without issue, his lawful brother Edmond, put back before, was admitted to the crowne').[10] It is, therefore, not impossible – indeed perhaps likely – that the unnamed king of *Thorney Abbey*, who is succeeded by a brother named Edmund, is meant to be Athelstan, with the king's own illegitimacy deflected onto that of his brother's fictional bastard heir. It might perhaps be some slight confirmation that Athelstan is certainly mentioned in one of the other plays published alongside *Thorney Abbey* in *Gratiae Theatrales*, William Haughton's *Grim the Collier of Croyden*, which seems to be connected to *Thorney Abbey* by more than just collocation because Edmund in *Thorney Abbey* is given the unhistorical title of Earl of London and so too is Morgan in *Grim the Collier*, and the two plays also share thunder effects and the motif of a liaison between a king and a nun.

I have suggested elsewhere that along with the anonymous *Guy of Warwick*, which is difficult to date but may possibly belong to the 1590s, and Dekker's *Old Fortunatus* (1599), *The Welsh Embassador* turned to Athelstan because it found in him a flexible, suggestive and culturally resonant figure who could be used to discuss a number of important issues, including succession, the status of the monarch and the relationship of early modern English identities to the histories which had produced them. Paul Hill declares that 'when history was re-written again in the Tudor period, Athelstan was all but lost', something which Hill is inclined to attribute to 'the fact that the Tudor line traced itself from the very dynasty which Athelstan had all but crushed',[11] but Athelstan was in his day a hugely important figure; Camden calls him 'the first English King that brought this countrey absolute under his dominion',[12] and Drayton notes that Athelstan was the first English king to wear a crown (though Drayton regards the mythical Molmutius as the first *British* king to have done so).[13] In addition, Athelstan may or may not have been the first to actually undergo a coronation ceremony, at Kingston-upon Thames,[14] but certainly 'His reign is the first in which we have a numismatic portrayal of a crowned head';[15] in fact, we have numerous images of him crowned,[16] including several which were in the possession of Sir Robert Cotton and so could have been known to Jacobean and Caroline writers. Sarah Foot remarks on a poem in praise of Athelstan found in a Cotton MS and on the fact that 'Leland reported that he had seen several books at Bath with inscriptions reporting their donation by AEthelstan', and notes too that Cotton owned a miniature of Athelstan with St Cuthbert which is now lost,[17] while Leland's *Itinerary* declares that Athelstan gave the borough of Barnstaple its privileges and that he gave an estate in Pilton to Malmesbury Abbey.[18] Cotton also had coins of Athelstan and possessed a book in which Athelstan is referred to as 'Anglorum basilyeos et curagulus totius Brytanniae'.[19] The celibate Athelstan also provided a potentially powerful lens for examining the benefits and logic of a celibate lifestyle as practised by monks and nuns, something which would be suggestive in the context of *Thorney Abbey*.

Besides Edmund, other characters in *Thorney Abbey* also have names to which we should attend. Munro notes that the play ignores Holinshed's association of Westminster Abbey with the mythical King Lucius,[20] supposedly the first Christian ruler of England, but it does give the name Lucius to the Bishop of London, and the wife of Earl Sibert of Coventry is called Emma, which was the name of a powerful Anglo-Saxon queen who was the wife of King

Canute and mother of both Hardicanute and (through her first marriage to Ethelred the Unready) of Edward the Confessor. Canute was a Christian who felt the need to adopt the baptismal name Lambert to signal a break with his Viking heritage; Edward the Confessor was a Catholic saint, so between them, Queen Emma's husband and son spanned a wide spectrum of religious identities. The play also contains an Earl of Wiltshire, the title bestowed upon Anne Boleyn's father Thomas (who survived her fall) and one of many hints that we ought to be thinking not only about the Anglo-Saxon period but also about the causes and effects of the English Reformation.

Thorney Abbey opens with the king, who describes himself in true Elizabethan fashion as making a 'progress' (sig. A1v), arriving to visit Sibert, who complains about the amount of people who want to present petitions on the occasion. The king intends to redress any wrongs he encounters, and Wiltshire warns him that he will find plenty:

> since you came
> From your Court at London still you see
> Corruption like a loathsome leprosy
> Hath made the faire face of ag'd ancestry
> Deform'd and hatefull. Temples, erected only
> To holy uses, are now for thrift turnd into barnes and stables.
> (sig. A1v)

Hearing this, Prince Edmund comments, "Twere fit for to reform them' (sig. A2r). 'Reform' here is a term both evocative and evasive: the Anglo-Saxon Prince Edmund obviously cannot be thinking of the Dissolution of the Monasteries, but the fact that the Earl of Wiltshire shares his title with the father of Anne Boleyn smuggles in a signpost pointing in that direction. Again there is a parallel with *Grim the Collier*, whose subtitle draws attention to the important role played by St Dunstan in the play, and there may be a background connection here, because Francis Young notes that 'King Edmund I appointed Dunstan abbot of Glastonbury in the 940s' and that Archbishop Dunstan 'told Abbo the hitherto unknown story of Edmund's death, which Dunstan in turn had heard, many years earlier, from a "decrepit old man" at the court of King AEthelstan'.[21] The connection between Dunstan and Athelstan is affirmed in *Grim the Collier* when the ghost of St Dunstan says that when he was alive

> I flourish'd in the reign of Seven great Kings;
> The first was Adelstane, whose Neece Elflida
> Malicious tongues reported, I defiled.
> (p. 3)

However, *Grim the Collier* also has St Dunstan's ghost claim that his power, although spiritually based, had in fact been effectively temporal in nature:

> With all these Kings was I in high esteem,
> And kept both them, and all the Land in awe;
> And, had I liv'd, the Danes had never boasted
> Their then beginning Conquest of this Land.
> (pp. 3–4)

Dunstan figures himself as not only the spiritual guide of kings but the political guardian of England, nicely showcasing the attitude that provoked Henry II to rid himself of his turbulent Archbishop Becket and Henry VIII to break with Rome and declare himself head of the English church. However, Dunstan also acknowledges that his sway was considered suspect by some:

> Yet some accuse me for a Conjurer,
> By reason of those many miracles
> Which Heaven for holy life endowed me with.
> But who so looks into the golden Legend,
> (That sacred Register of holy Saints)
> Shall find me by the Pope canoniz'd.
> (p. 4)

Unfortunately, most people in post-Reformation England would not be particularly reassured by the information that this is a saint who has been canonised by the Pope, and this is also a dilemma faced by *Thorney Abbey*.

When Earl Sibert hears that the unnamed king of *Thorney Abbey* plans to redress the wrongs of his people, he decides to kill him, though his wife Emma takes the lead in the proceedings and hides the king's corpse in a river bed. Meanwhile, the king's brother Prince Edmund seduces Thorney's daughter Anne with the aid of a ring he has begged from her father but promises to marry her; however, he is called away by his brother's death and a visibly pregnant Anne is cast out by her father despite the pleas of her cousin Woodford, to whom she confesses Edmund's identity. Thorney orders Anne to be whipped and vows to leave his money to the church, but Woodford saves her from the whipping and takes her to his own house. Although Edmund seemed sincere when he vowed to return for her, he is distracted both by the need to identify his brother's killer and by the fact that neither sun nor moon has shone since the murder nor has the thunder stopped. He heads for Coventry, much to the distress of Sibert, who, racked with guilt, resolves to flee to Ireland (though in fact he is prevented by storms). His flight leads

Wiltshire to accuse Emma and suggest that her hands are red with the king's blood; she denies it but is understandably shaken when a blazing star appears and points at her, upon which she confesses and dies. Edmund condemns the captured Sibert and the two murderers to be impaled on stakes; the corpse of Emma is to be burned, the body of the king is recovered from the river bed, and the sun and moon shine again. An early modern audience would have understood that the fact that the king's body is retrieved and decently reburied has implications not only for the king's own spiritual journey but for his successor too: Nicole Marafioti argues that 'kings used royal graves to reinforce the idea that they had been selected by God to rule',[22] and Peter Ross regards Westminster Abbey as fundamentally linked to Edward the Confessor's decision to be both crowned and buried there: 'the abbey's fame and meaning have derived from these twin roles as royal burial place and crowning place, a church of bones and thrones'.[23]

Meanwhile, Anne's child is born and she enters the convent at Holywell, leaving a message entrusting the infant Edmund to his father. Five years pass and Anne's father Old Thorney retreats into religious life; a dumb show shows '*Thorny with Cittizens, giving them large summes of money: shewing them the money: desires them to see his building goe forward: takes his leave with a deaths head in his hand: goes into the tombe*', which is identified as being 'a mile from London' (p. 41). His servant Lobster feeds him while he lives there and when he hears that Anne has become a nun, he sends her the skull as a token of forgiveness. A second dumb show sees Edmund being finally reminded of Anne's existence, upon which he determines to visit her. The bishop rules that he can only do this if he dons religious clothing:

> For ne're no man, unless a frier in confession,
> Might meet in private with a sacred Nunne.
> (p. 46)

There is an obvious parallel here with *Measure for Measure*, where Isabella too has physically passed from literal temporal to spiritual space, and the Duke, disguised as a friar, outrageously hears her confession. There is also a similar outcome: just as the Duke proposes to Isabella, so Edmund, moved by the sight of Anne and also by that of his son, announces that he will marry her. This may seem a happy ending, but there are some potentially troubling overtones to the idea of a king dressing up as a cleric and infiltrating a monastery: Thomas Williams observes of King Constantine of Dumnonia that 'Gildas [...] accused him of killing two youths in church before the holy dais [...] If that were not bad enough, Constantine himself was at the time apparently clothed "in the habit of a holy abbot"'.[24] Finally, Old Thorney is visited in sleep by an angel who conducts him around the abbey he has funded and then wakened by his grandson, now legitimised and acknowledged as heir to the throne; forgiving Anne and renouncing the world, he dies, leaving Thorney Abbey to carry on his name.

The play presents the founding of Thorney Abbey as emotionally fraught since Old Thorney lavishes his money and energy on it once he has cast out his daughter, but unproblematic in practical terms; at the end of the play, spiritual and temporal lands are neatly apportioned and the young Edmund shows no signs of coveting the land his grandfather has gifted away. But the subsequent history of Westminster Abbey was not in fact quite so simple and trouble-free, and that leaches into the play. Munro argues that '*Thorney Abbey* reworks a historical narrative, in this case that of the Saxon abbey and its founder. In doing so, it attempts to efface the religious turmoil and trauma of the Reformation and to present Anglo-Saxon religious practices as a mirror image of those of the Jacobean Church of England'. However, she notes that the attempt does not succeed: 'religious identity in *Thorney Abbey* is fundamentally ambiguous, the product of an incomplete process of dissolution and reformation'.[25] This is partly because the play's depiction of the interplay between temporal and spiritual jurisdictions was set against a troubled background. As the name Emma may remind us, the land on which Westminster Abbey now stands may also have been the scene of a boundary dispute of an existential kind: before the Thames was embanked, this was Thorney Island (the real source of the abbey's original name), and it is reputed to have been the place where Canute showed his courtiers that he could not turn back the tide. It was certainly where he built his Palace of Westminster, which Nicole Marafioti thinks was his preferred royal residence,[26] and even today, the official website of the Houses of Parliament records irritation at the fact that 'The awkward site occupied by the early palace buildings at Westminster was because the Abbey church was already built on the best land on the island'.[27] The anger cut both ways: Jeremy Ashbee notes that 'The 15th-century "Black Book" of Westminster Abbey recorded the monks' anger at the seizure of their land for the construction of the Jewel Tower and its moat, and the divine retribution that struck the perpetrator', William Usshborne.[28] Since their inception, the communities of this now-invisible island have seen secular and spiritual powers jostling for space.

Although this uneasy cohabitation is not officially registered in *Thorney Abbey*, the play does parallel the idea of battle over an island by offering three striking instances of fluids failing to stick to their courses. When Prince Edmund first falls in lust with Anne Thorney, he admits,

I know that my desire is ill; yet cannot I
Desist from my foul purpose; for my bounded course

> Of humane reason overflowes their banks,
> And runs disorderedly through all my vaines.
> (sig. A5r)

The river to which Edmund refers here is only a metaphorical one, but soon a real river is being diverted when Emma comes up with a cunning plan for concealing the corpse of the king:

> Know this my Lord; here by the uncouth cavern of a wall,
> A solitary brook doth glide along,
> Which we have turn'd from forth his proper course,
> And in the mid'st o'th channel digg'd a pit,
> Where when the murdred King is once intomb'd,
> The nimble current shall be brought again,
> And overrun the royall Sepulchre.
> (sig. A6r)

Nicole Marafioti explains that King Harthacnut, son of the historical Queen Emma and King Canute, had his predecessor Harold Harefoot (who claimed to be his half-brother) disinterred from his grave in Westminster and either 'thrown into a swamp' or 'dumped in the Thames', but 'a number of his subjects directly defied their new king by retrieving the disinterred body and reburying it in an appropriate, consecrated grave';[29] Marafioti notes that 'The earliest record of Harold's exhumation appears in Manuscript C of the Anglo-Saxon Chronicle',[30] and the story may have featured in the lost play *Hardicanute*.[31] The Emma of the play will not only kill a virtuous and pious king but will deny him Christian burial, something which could potentially affect his soul as well as his body: Marafioti notes that 'Intramurial burial at Westminster [had] distinguished Harold [Harefoot] from the ranks of ordinary Christian dead and secured the attention of the monastic community entrusted with praying for his soul',[32] and Alexandra Walsham observes that 'In Monmouthshire in the 1690s, the papists of the parish of St Maughan remained "very eager to be brought to be buried" in the church, believing it would ensure their "communication through ye purgatory"'.[33] The swamp (or section of the Thames) into which the real Harold Harefoot's body was allegedly thrown is echoed in the play by the depositing of the murdered king in a diverted river bed, and there is a third instance of disordered waters when Sibert is unable to reach Ireland because 'the mounting waves […] would not beare a Kings base murtherer' (p. 39). Thorney Island might no longer have been discernable as an island and disputes over its tightly confined space might have been in abeyance, but the play repeatedly evokes disturbed and disturbing watercapes.

Moreover, as early as the Prelude, the play itself embarks on a boundary dispute of sorts:

A Prelude to THORNY-ABBEY.
Enter a Fool with a Paper in his hand for a Prologue.
Fool.
HA! ha! I'me come now *at last*, or *at first*, which you will: for I am *first* here. D'ye call't a *Tragedy*? so they tell me it is, and that no *fools* must be in *Tragedies*: for they are *serious* matters, forsooth. But I say there may, and there must be *fools* in *Tragedies,* and you call them *Tragedies,* or there will be no *Tragedies.* And I tell you more, they are all *fools* in the *Tragedy*; and you are *fools,* that come to see the *Tragedy*; and the *Poet*'s a *fool,* who made the *Tragedy,* to tell a Story of a King and a Court, and leave a *fool* out on't; when in *Pacy*'s, and *Sommers*'s and *Patche*'s, and *Archer*'s times, my venerable Predecessours, a *fool* was alwayes the *Principal Verb*; and, as I suppose, was so too long before that; and, as I suppose, when *Thorny* built his *Abbey* too; I, and as I suppose, we shall by his good leave, or without it, continue so still to the end of the Chapter. But, now I talk of the *Principal Verb,* I have a *part* to say to you, if the *Prompter* would come to tell me, when I am out.

This speech acknowledges a territorial dispute between different genres and also breaks the fourth wall by its references to real fools and its reminder of the existence of a prompter, whose services are in fact almost immediately required and who batters an even bigger hole in the fourth wall when he dismisses the Fool as 'unready in's part' before going on to explain that the subject of the play is

> To shew how *Royal* bloud's reveng'd when spilt,
> And *THORNY-Abbey* first came to be built,
> A place for great devotion of much fame,
> Which since to *Westminster* hath chang'd its name.
> (EEBO image 7)

The suggestive word 'Unready' recalls the adjective notoriously applied to King Ethelred, whose son Edward the Confessor was the official founder of Westminster Abbey. Lucy Munro notes that 'the Saxon Thorney Abbey functions as the bottom layer of an anachronistic palimpsest, overlaid and overwritten by the later abbey with which the play's audiences would have been familiar';[34] evoking Ethelred the Unready reminds us of some of the more disruptive aspects of the historical changes which have shaped that palimpsest and also point up the fact that there may be more than one version of the past.

This is further underlined by the fact that when it comes to the murder of the king, *Thorney Abbey* is visibly drawing not on history but on *Macbeth*. Sibert's wife Emma hires two murderers and the killing is carried out to the accompaniment of thunder before a discovery-of-the-crime scene modelled in virtually every detail on *Macbeth*, down to Sibert's killing of the late king's pages. This coupling of Saxon kings with memories of *Macbeth* puts pressure on Shakespeare's play, and I think particularly on its use of Edward the Confessor. If Shakespeare had indeed seen the Wilton Diptych, as is suggested by *Richard II*, he would have been aware that Edward the Confessor and St Edmund stand side by side on the left-hand panel, and he would certainly have known that they had adjacent chapels in Westminster Abbey. He would thus have been well aware that Edward was both a king, whose reputed crown and chair were both used in the coronation ceremonies of Tudor and Stuart monarchs (including that of James I in 1603), and also a saint, having been canonised in 1161. Edward the Confessor's sacred monarchy seems the polar opposite of Macbeth's impious and witch-assisted reign, but as a saint, he was suspect in Protestant eyes; the practice of touching for the king's evil, for which Edward is specifically commended in *Macbeth*, was eschewed by James I, and Malcolm's assurance that 'He hath a heavenly gift of prophecy' (4.3.157) might also ring alarm bells in a play in which most of the prophesying is done by the three Weird Sisters. It is therefore suggestive that although Malcolm asks 'Comes the King forth, I pray you?' and the Doctor answers 'Ay, sir',[35] he does not actually appear. There is, however, a covert reminder of the importance of Westminster Abbey itself in *Macbeth*'s three references to Scone (2.4.31 and 35, 5.9.41), since the so-called Stone of Scone (properly the Stone of Destiny) had sat in a niche under Edward the Confessor's coronation chair since the reign of Edward I, in token of English monarchs' claim to suzerainty over Scotland. *Macbeth* treads a nervous line between implying the superiority of a king who collapses the distinction between spiritual and temporal and refusing to actually show him.

Macbeth nods to the importance of other religious establishments and figures and perhaps even other faiths: Duncan's body is carried to 'Colmekill' (2.4.33), that is the Abbey of Iona founded by St Columba, and Todd Andrew Borlik notes that 'the name of the Duncan character in Holinshed is Duffe, an early modern spelling of dove, while the name of his son Malcolm signifies 'devotee of St Columba'.[36] Moreover, Céline Savatier-Lahondès suggests that

> The Weird Sisters in Shakespeare's *Macbeth* echo the three druidesses and the motif of the warrior tree is present in the *Second Battle of Moytura*

in the Irish mythological Cycle, in the *Mabinogi of Branwen*, daughter of Lir and in the Welsh poem of the *Kat Godeu* or *Fight of the Little Trees*. It is difficult to overlook the parallel with *Macbeth*, in which the three Weird Sisters prophesy the movement of Birnam wood to the fortress of Dunsinane.[37]

This potential evocation of Celtic mythology might remind us that St Columba's abbey of Iona had originally represented not only a different national religious centre but also a significantly different form of Celtic Christianity, with distinct customs and structures. Ostensibly *Macbeth* exalts the figure of Edward the Confessor and by implication his foundation, but in fact it fights shy of the saint and reminds us that Westminster Abbey is not the only traditional site of royal burials and coronations.

Macbeth also offers disturbing commentary on the vexed boundary between temporal and spiritual spheres. Having first figured himself as keeping 'Hell Gate' (2.3.2), the Porter fantasises that 'here's an equivocator that could swear in both the scales against either scale, who committed treason enough for God's sake, yet could not equivocate to heaven' (2.3.8–11). As many critics have observed, this glances at the trials of the Gunpowder Plot conspirators, which had publicised the fact that Jesuits licensed equivocation. The Porter himself in some sense equivocates by conflating treason, a political crime, and faith, though at the same time, he alienates faith from itself by implying that the religious convictions of the traitors cut no ice with heaven. Moreover, he himself is both a literal figure, the real porter of a real castle, and yet also an allegorical one, in ways which simultaneously position him and invest him with authority within both the spiritual and the temporal spheres. Well may he say 'I pray you, remember the porter' (2.3.19–20); we should indeed remember a figure who sheds such powerful light upon the play's ideological workings by drawing attention to the troubled interplay between the power of the state and the power of the church.

Between them, then, *Thorney Abbey* and *Macbeth*, with a little help from *Grim the Collier of Croyden*, plot a very tentative boundary between temporal and spiritual authority but highlight its vulnerability and the potential for bleed between the two. All three plays display particular nervousness around the question of how virtuous kings need to be, and the extent to which their rule can be conceived of as sacred or as divinely sanctioned, as well as the extent to which others (including prelates) can counsel or reprove them, all obviously questions which resonated loudly after the accession of James I, author of *The True Law of Free Monarchies* and firm believer in divine right. The king in *Thorney Abbey* is entirely virtuous, but before the play is very old, he is also entirely dead, and his slightly less virtuous brother is a great deal more successful. King Duncan in *Macbeth* is another good ruler who is killed early on, while Malcolm unsettlingly echoes the witches' truth-like lies by lying about himself to prove his truth and worth to rule. As Macbeth's porter keeps both the gate of hell and the gate of Dunsinane while an angel leads the grandfather of the future king round the perimeter of the future Westminster Abbey, spiritual and temporal lands lie side by side in an unquiet and ominous peace.

Notes

1 Nicole Marafioti, *The King's Body: Burial and Succession in Late Anglo-Saxon England* (Toronto: University of Toronto Press, 2014), p. 242.
2 (London: R. D. 1662).
3 Lucy Munro, '"Nemp your sexes!": Anachronistic Aesthetics in *Hengist, King of Kent* and the Jacobean "Anglo-Saxon" Play', *Modern Philology* 111. 4 (May 2014), pp. 734–61, p. 741, note 18 and p. 736.
4 Francis Young, *Edmund: In Search of England's Lost King* [2018] (London: Bloomsbury, 2021), pp. 110–11, 122, 127, 128 and 131.
5 Young, *Edmund*, pp. 103 and 105.
6 Munro, "Nemp your sexes!", p. 738.
7 Lisa Hopkins, 'Athelstan: The Virgin King', in *From the Romans to the Normans on the English Renaissance Stage* (UK: ARC Humanities Press, 2017).
8 Sarah Foot, *Athelstan: The First King of England* (New Haven and London: Yale University Press, 2011), p. 91.
9 Foot, *Athelstan*, p. 12.
10 Robert Persons, *A Conference About the Next Succession to the Crowne of Ingland* (Antwerp: A. Conincx, 1595), pp. 181–2.
11 Paul Hill, *The Age of Athelstan: Britain's Forgotten History* [2004] (Stroud: The History Press, 2008), pp. 16 and 206.
12 William Camden, *Britain*, translated by Philemon Holland (London: F. Kingston, R. Young and J. Legatt for George Latham, 1637), p. 196.
13 Michael Drayton, *Poly-Olbion or a Chorographicall Description of Tracts, Riuers, Mountains, Forests, and Other Parts of this Renowned Isle of Great Britain* (London: Augustine Mathewes, 1622), p. 108.
14 It is sometimes claimed that his father, Edward the Elder, underwent such a ceremony, but Sarah Foot thinks Athelstan, not Edward the Elder, was the first monarch to be crowned at Kingston (Foot, *Athelstan*, p. 74).
15 Hill, *The Age of Athelstan*, p. 121.
16 See for instance Foot, *Athelstan*, p. 77.
17 Foot, *Athelstan*, pp. 94, 119 and 121.
18 John Chandler, *John Leland's Itinerary: Travels in Tudor England* (Stroud: Alan Sutton, 1993), pp. 106–7.
19 Foot, *Athelstan*, pp. 154–5 and 212.
20 Munro, "Nemp your sexes!", p. 757, note 62.
21 Young, *Edmund*, pp. 83 and 51.
22 Marafioti, *The King's Body*, p. 25.

23 Peter Ross, *Steeple Chasing: Around Britain by Church*, 2nd ed (London: Headline, 2024), p. 360.
24 Thomas Williams, *Lost Realms: Histories of Britain from the Romans to the Vikings* (London: William Collins, 2022), p. 154.
25 Munro, "Nemp your sexes!", pp. 739 and 759.
26 Marafioti, *The King's Body*, p. 217.
27 https://www.parliament.uk/about/living-heritage/building/palace/estatehistory/the-middle-ages/anglosaxon-royal-palace/.
28 Jeremy Ashbee, *Guidebook: The Jewel Tower* (English Heritage, n.d.), p. 16.
29 Marafioti, *The King's Body*, pp. 126–7; see also p. 144.
30 Marafioti, *The King's Body*, p. 144.
31 https://lostplays.folger.edu/Hardicanute_(Canute).
32 Marafioti, *The King's Body*, p. 148.
33 Alexandra Walsham, *The Reformation of the Landscape: Religion, Identity, and Memory in Early Modern Britain and Ireland* (Oxford: Oxford University Press, 2011), p. 175.
34 Munro, "Nemp your sexes!", p. 739.
35 William Shakespeare, *Macbeth*, edited by Sandra Clark and Pamela Mason (London: Bloomsbury Arden Shakespeare, 2015), 4.3.140–1. All subsequent quotations from the play will be taken from this edition and reference will be given in the text.
36 Todd Andrew Borlik, *Shakespeare Beyond the Green World: Drama and Ecopolitics in Jacobean Britain* (Oxford: Oxford University Press, 2023), p. 41.
37 Céline Savatier-Lahondès, 'The Reconstruction of an Ancient Past in Shakespeare's Drama', *Études écossaises* 20 (2018), pp. 1–20, p. 7.

Chapter 2

A KNACK TO KNOW A KNAVE

The anonymous play *A Knack to Know a Knave* was first performed on 10 June 1592 and published in 1594, although Hanspeter Born has argued that the version published was not identical to the one performed but had been revised by Shakespeare.[1] It features Bishop Dunstan, who was initially Abbot of Glastonbury, subsequently Archbishop of Canterbury, and finally canonised, and Edgar, king of Mercia and Northumbria (c. 944–975), who was known as Edgar the Peaceful. Both Edgar and Dunstan carried considerable cultural heft. Dunstan was a complex and controversial figure who meant very different things at different periods: his association with miracles that savoured of trickery meant that to early Reformers he was even more suspect than most saints. Paul H. Kocher observes that a marginal note in Henry Holland's 1590 *A Treatise Against Witchcraft* couples 'Faustus' and 'Drunken Dunstan' and posits that although '*Drunken Dunstan* eludes identification', 'No doubt it is some sort of attack on Dunstan, to whom, with other Catholic saints, Protestants gave a reputation for dissoluteness and magic';[2] however, Alexandra Walsham observes that 'As time progressed and passions attenuated it even became possible to rejuvenate parts of the legends of saints like St Dunstan, whom an earlier generation of polemicists had refashioned as the archetype of the proud prelate, worker of lying wonders, and arrogant usurper of temporal authority'.[3]

Edgar was also a contested figure. As we see in *A Knack to Know a Knave*, he figured in a story about lust and murder, but he was the subject of two panegyrics in the *Anglo-Saxon Chronicle*, preserved in a manuscript which Mercedes Salvador-Bello observes was in the Cotton collection and so accessible to at least some early modern readers,[4] and he too was canonised because 'In 1052 AEthelweard, abbot of Glastonbury, opened King Edgar's grave and found his body to be incorrupt; it was then placed in a silver-gilt casket, over the altar, with relics of St Apollinaris and St Vincent, and miracles followed'.[5] Edgar's son, his daughter and one of his wives were also canonised. The reign of Edgar (whose father Edmund was Athelstan's half-brother and successor) saw a brief respite from the wave of Viking invasions but England saw troubled times again as his eldest son Edward the Martyr was murdered at Corfe Castle (allegedly by his stepmother Aelfthryth) and succeeded by his half-brother Ethelred the Unready. *A Knack to Know a Knave* is to the best of my knowledge the only early modern play to feature Edgar (unless one takes literally the fact that a character named Edgar appears to succeed to the throne at the end of *King Lear*), but *John a Kent and John a Cumber* mentions him being rowed on the Dee by eight kings (ll. 160–72), which Manley and Maclean argue suggests that it, like *A Knack to Know a Knave*, was a Strange's Men play.[6]

Edgar's main achievement was the revival of Benedictine monasticism. Peter Rex argues that 'Monastic bishops, largely introduced by Edgar, supported by the abbots of newly revived or re-founded monasteries, proved to be the pillars of Edgar's reign'; for Rex, it is partly as a result of this that 'Edgar [...] deserves the accolade of being the first unchallenged King of England'.[7] Edgar was certainly a strong ruler: Rex notes that 'his ealdormen and nobles acquiesced without recorded demur in the revival of Benedictine monasticism and the transfer of large quantities of landed property to the hands of monastic communities', and he even succeeded in getting inland parishes to help pay for ships, the issue which would eventually break Charles I.[8] Rex adds that 'Edgar enforced the payment of *Romefeoli* or Peter's Pence, also called hearth penny, an offering of alms for the upkeep of the papacy', although after he died 'there occurred what most historians have termed an "anti-monastic reaction"'.[9] Edgar can thus be seen as almost the perfect test case for considering the relationship between temporal and spiritual power. Donna Hamilton notes that in his revisions to *Acts and Monuments* Foxe argued that 'the notorious King Edgar further contaminated the church, for during his time, "the multitude of monks began fyrst to swarme in the churches of England" (r5r)', and when the Protestant Sir Edward Coke argued that 'the king held both ecclesiastical and temporal power', Robert Persons argued against this and cited Edgar in support.[10]

A Knack to Know a Knave opens with Edgar declaring his determination to be a good king who rules according to the law of God, and congratulating himself on his success so far:

> DVnston, how highlie are we bound to praise
> The Eternall God that still prouides for vs,
> And giues vs leaue to rule in this our land
> [...]
> First, murther we rewarde with present death,
> And those that doe commit fellonious crimes,
> Our lawes of England doe awarde them death:

And he that doeth dispoyle a Uirgins chastitie,
Must lykewise suffer death by lawes decree,
And that decree is trreuocable.
Then as I am Gods Uicegerent here on earth,
By Gods appointment heere to raigne and rule,
So must I seeke to cut abuses downe.¹¹

Implicitly subscribing to the theory of the divine right of kings, Edgar sees himself as 'Gods Uicegerent' or deputy wielder of power, by whom the rule of law is unswervingly upheld: murder and rape are invariably punished with death, though there do seem to be unspecified surviving 'abuses' which Edgar must still 'seeke to cut [...] downe' (the play will later have plenty to say about what those might be, but at the moment they seem to constitute only a marginal issue).

Dunstan entirely concurs that this is a golden age for the country:

Your Graces care herein I much cummend,
And England hath iust cause to praise the Lorde,
That sent so good a King to gouerne them.
(sig. A2r)

There doesn't seem much prospect of narrative development at this point if England is already a Utopia, but there is an unexpected intervention from a speaker named only as 'Honesty':

And yet thou art not happy Edgar,
Because that sinnes, lyke swarmes, remaine in thee.
(sig. A3r)

The King dismisses Honesty as a 'base Peasant' (sig. A3r) who has displeased him, but Honesty is not cowed and tells the King that he is a victim of flattery while he himself possesses 'a Knacke to know a Knaue' (sig. A3r), upon which King Edgar licenses him as a sort of knave-finder general. Edgar also asks Honesty what motivates him, the response to which offers some biting social satire:

If I shuld tel your Grace twold make you laugh
To heare how Honesty was entertainde,
Poore, lame and blinde when I came once ashore,
Lord, how they came in flocks to visit me,
The shepheard with his hooke, and Thrasher with his flaile,

> The very pedler with his dog, and the tinker with his male.
> Then comes a souldier counterfeit, & with him was his Iug,
> And Wil the whipper of the dogs had got a bounsing trug:
> And coging Dick was in the crue, that swore he cam frō Frāce
> He swore that in the Kings defence, he lost his arm by chance,
> And yet in conscience, if I were put to sweare,
> I would be bound to lay a pound, the knaue was neuer there,
> And hapning mongst this companie by chance one day,
> I had no sooner namde my name, but they ran all away.
> (sig. A4r)

Honesty has apparently travelled from overseas, since his first encounter with Edgar's subjects was when he 'came [...] ashore', and is greeted by a social spectrum reminiscent of something out of Chaucer or *Piers Plowman*: a shepherd, a thresher, a pedlar, a tinker, a drunken braggart soldier, a huntsman and a beggar who pretends to have been maimed in the French wars all flock to see him until they hear his name, Honesty, and promptly flee because none of them have anything to do with honesty. Despite Edgar's confidence in the perfection of his own rule, there is apparently quite a lot wrong with the state of his England.

Having thus made his point Honesty then leaves, as does the courtier Perin, who has asked leave to visit his sick father (the audience being implicitly invited to wonder whether Perin's departure is coincidental or whether he too wants nothing to do with honesty). Left alone with Dunstan, Edgar now reveals a rather less amiable side to his nature, telling Dunstan that he has heard of a beautiful girl named Alfrida whom he would like to make his mistress. Dunstan replies that he could not countenance anything less than marriage, upon which the king objects that he cannot marry a girl he has never seen and despatches Earl Ethenwald, Dunstan's nephew, to look her over.

The scene then abruptly shifts to the northern town of Hexham, site of a decisive battle in the Wars of the Roses on 15 May 1464, which sounded the death knell of the house of Lancaster and saw the execution of the Duke of Somerset and the capture of Henry VI's treasury, and which seems to have formed the subject of a lost play by Barnabe Barnes.[12] King Edgar had no connection with the town (though he gave land both to Chester Cathedral and to the Archbishop of York), but Wilfrid's original foundation at Hexham belonged to Edgar's favoured Benedictine order (it became Augustinian only under the Normans). Perhaps, too, the name of the town appealed to the playwright, for 'Hexham' could be broken down into hex-ham, witch-town, and, as we shall see, the Hexham of the play is a distinctly uncanny place in which good spiritual forces tussle with bad ones. Anyone who wanted to detect such an etymology might well have been encouraged by the fact that the river which flowed past the town, on the banks of which the Battle of Hexham was fought, was named Devil's Water.

At the time the play was published, the status of Hexham had recently undergone a significant change when the Parliament of May–June 1572 passed an 'Acte for the annexing of Hexham and Hexhamshire to the Countie of Northumberland', noting that

> her maiestie yet is seased of and in the fraunchise and libertie of Hexham and Hexamshire, lying within the body and mydle of the Countie of Northumberlande, whiche sayde libertie & territorie, when it was in the handes of the sayde Archebishop [of York], was commonly tearmed & named a Countie Palentyne, where in ryght or proofe there was none suche, yet by reason of that errour, euer since, and yet, there hath ben, and are diuers opinions, besides some question and doubtes, whether the sayd libertie and territorie of Hexham and Hexhamshire, should and ought to be part of the sayde Countie of Northumberland, or otherwyse exempted [...] may it therefore please the queene her Maiestie, that by her highnesse, the lordes spiritual and temporal, & the commons in this present hygh court of Parliament nowe assembled, that it may be enacted, manifested, and declared by aucthoritie of the same, that the sayd territorie, fraunchise, and libertie of Hexham and Hexhamshire, with the liberties of the same, may be, is, and shalbe from henceefoorth taken to be within, and part, parcell and member of the sayd Countie of Northumberlande.[13]

A county palatine was an effectively autonomous region subject to the unchallenged authority of either a temporal magnate (in the case of the county palatine of Chester, governed by the earls of Chester) or a spiritual one (as was true of the county palatine of Durham, ruled by the bishops of Durham – called therefore the Prince Bishops – and known colloquially in the region as 'St Cuthbert's Land'). Chester and Durham were essentially the only two remaining by the Elizabethan period, the county of Lancaster having effectively lost its palatinate status after the Duchy was merged with the Crown following the accession of Henry IV; if Hexhamshire were to be recognised as a third substantive palatinate that would entail tacit acknowledgement that the Archbishop of York had temporal as well as spiritual powers. Even though the earls of Northumberland were considered highly untrustworthy by the Crown (one having led the rebellion of the northern earls in support of Mary Queen of Scots only three years before this Act came before parliament), it was clearly preferable to see the disputed territory subsumed within their domain rather than that of the Archbishop.

The Act declares that the purpose of the change it proposes is to rectify a situation in which

> not onely Plees of the Crowne, and suites betwixt partie & partie haue suffered continuall stayes, lets, and also haue had no ende of tryall, and besides, the most & greatest offendours to the crowne & their Countrey, haue, & dayly runne thither as vnto a sanctuarie, vpon hope and trust of refuge and safegarde thereby, to the great comfort and encouragement of many, the vilest & worste subiectes and offendours in all the North parties, and to the great offence of the almightie & most manifest hinderaunce of good execution of lawes and iustice.

The Act alleges that the rule of law has been suspended if not paralysed by the current uncertainty over whose writ should run in the region, and this seems to be reflected in *A Knack to Know a Knave* when we meet the bailiff of Hexham and his four sons, who are, respectively, a courtier, a coney-catcher, a priest and a farmer. The bailiff gives each of them advice about how to act fraudulently and hypocritically and create trouble, though by their own confessions, they all already seem to be managing perfectly well in this respect. Having finished his suggestions for ways in which his sons might do wrong the bailiff is seized by a devil and carried off to hell, his son John, who is a priest, being powerless to intervene because he has left his book at home and can't think of anything to say.

We then switch back to King Edgar, who is being asked to give judgement against his favoured courtier Philarchus for unfilial behaviour to his poverty-stricken father. Philarchus expresses regret for his past conduct, but his father will not forgive him and pleads for the death penalty. Unwilling to ratify this, Edgar appoints the father as judge in his place, and the father banishes Philarchus the realm, in a neat demonstration of how abstract principles of justice may falter in the face of personal considerations. This scene is followed by one in which Honesty detects the knavery of the coney-catcher, who is one of the four sons of the late bailiff of Hexham and is planning a complicated scam:

> I haue attyred my selfe lyke a very ciuill citizen,
> To drawe foure score pound from a couple of fooles,
> A Gentleman hauing made ouer his land by deed of gift,
> Means to cosen a broker with a false conueiance.
> (sig. C2r)

The plot hinges on the invalidity of the conveyance, which purports to offer some land as a guarantee in the event that a loan of 80 pounds fails to be repaid. The deal is in full swing when Honesty (now pretending to be Welsh and referring to himself as 'her' in the way that Welshmen supposedly did) intervenes:

> God saue her sirs, and her good friendes, is a poore Welshman, come as far as Carnaiuan in Wales to receiue a litle money, and here a has paid her I cannot tell what. Here you master, wat is it not brasse money? (sig. C3v)

Honesty's feigned Welshness enables him to mention Caernarfon, the castle whose conquest had proved the pretext for Edward I to confer the title of Prince of Wales on his eldest son; this might just be a rather subtle (possibly too subtle to be very effective) hint at the question of succession, since King Edgar is still only at the stage of thinking about marriage (and seems more interested in taking a mistress than a wife). Honesty does not prevent the fraudulent deal but does reveal that he understands it; he also addresses the coney-catcher as Cuthbert, placing him firmly in the north of England and connecting him to the region's most famous saint, and he brings the king, in disguise, to observe the coney-catcher's false dealing, after which the king orders him to be branded on the forehead so that everyone will know him for a criminal. After the revelation of the incapacity of the first son, a priest, to save their father, a second of the bailiff's sons is thus neutralised.

This scene is counterpointed by one in which a knight (not previously seen and identified only by his rank) remarks to Walter, third of the bailiff's sons and a farmer,

> Neighbour Walter I cannot but admire to see
> How housekeeping is decayed within this thirtie yeare,
> But where the fault is God knowes, I knowe not:
> My father in his lyfe time gaue hospitality to all strangers, and
> Distressed traueillers, his table was neuer emptie of bread, beefe
> And beere, he was woont to keep a hundred tall men in his hall.
> He was a feaster of all commers in generall,
> And yet was he neuer in want of money:
> I thinke God did blesse him with increase, for his bountiful mind
> (sigs D2r-D3v)

This lament would have had considerable contemporary resonance; Todd Andrew Borlik cites a 1606 petition as lamenting a vanished world in which

'Noblemen and gentlemen were wont to keep two hundred persons in their houses daily ready to serve the king',[14] and the general understanding was that any significant gentry household would act as a support centre and a site of hospitality for the neighbourhood in general.

Walter, however, has no time for this old-fashioned belief in the value of being of service to society. Instead, he advises the knight to stop trying to emulate his father and to cut costs wherever he can:

> Keepe but a boy or two within your house,
> To run of errants, and to wait on you,
> And for your kitchin, keep a woman cooke,
> One that will serue for thirtie shillings a yeare:
> And by that means you saue two liueries,
> And if ye will keep retainers towards you,
> Let them be Farmers, or rich husbandmen,
> For you shal find great profit (sir) in keeping them:
> For if you stand in need of corne or hay,
> Send but to them, and you may haue it strait:
> And if you kill a Beefe, let it be so leane
> The Butcher nor the Grasyer will not buy it,
> Your drinke is too strong, and tastes too much of malt,
> Tush, single beere is better far, both for your profit, and your seruants health
> And at a Christmasse time feast none at al,
> But such as yeeld you some commoditie:
> I meane such as will send you now and then,
> Fat Geese and Capons to keep house withall,
> To these and none els would I haue you liberall.
> (sig. D3v)

The knight objects that this is not the ethos of knighthood – 'Why neighbor, my goods are lent me to no other end / But to releeue my needie brethren' (sigs D3v-r) – and subsequently does his best to arbitrate in a dispute between two local poor men; however, when they are both requested by Perin (of whom more in a moment) to provide loans for the king, Walter the farmer proves able to offer ten times the amount that the knight can manage. In return, Walter demands the right to export corn overseas to maximise his profit (and by implication to starve his neighbours), even though this will 'mak[e] poore Piers ploughman weare a thread bare coate' [sig. C3v]). Once again Honesty exposes Walter and also demonstrates the venality of his brother the priest; as a final flourish, he proves the corruption of Perin, the courtier who left in the first scene to see his dying father and who now turns out to be not only the fourth son of the bailiff but also the judge who convicted the coney-catcher and the fund-raiser who asked for money from the knight and Walter. All four sons of the bailiff thus meet their just deserts at the hands of Honesty.

Meanwhile, Ethenwald has predictably wooed Alfrida for himself rather than for the king, whom he fobs off by an assurance that she is not really very beautiful until Perin spills the beans. Edgar therefore decides to visit Ethenwald and his new wife; Ethenwald assumes that he must mean to seduce her and resolves that Alfrida shall swap places with Kate the kitchen maid, but Edgar detects the deception and dooms Ethenwald to death. Determined to save his nephew, Dunstan conjures up the devil Asmoroth, whom he orders to impersonate Ethenwald, but the king remembers that adultery is bad and pardons the earl in any case. All those whom Honesty has shown to be guilty are condemned to death, and everyone else presumably lives happily ever after.

This story is completely unhistorical: the original of Ethenwald seems to have died of natural causes – Rex observes that 'There is no evidence that Ealdorman Aethewold died violently [...] Aethelwold simply died sometime before 964, the year in which the king married his widow'[15] – and Edgar did in fact marry Alfrida. It seems even more improbable that Dunstan, who became Archbishop of Canterbury and has a good claim to be one of the most beloved English saints in the mediaeval period, should conjure up the Devil. Tom Rutter observes that 'While a variety of images of Dunstan were available to Elizabethan dramatists, ranging from the saintly to the almost satanic, the playwright (or playwrights) responsible for *A Knack to Know a Knave* apparently chose the frivolous version discarded in the chronicles, an upright man who is on terms with devils, while firmly retaining both the upper hand and his spiritual integrity'.[16] This tolerance of a saint's dalliance with demons might seem surprising, but Lawrence Manley and Sally Beth Maclean see *A Knack to Know a Knave* as participating in 'a strand of antipuritan satire that was perhaps the earliest and strongest on the Elizabethan stage', seen here in a mode which is already implicitly redolent of Catholic England, 'a reenactment of the Last Judgement in the cycle plays'.[17]

The introduction of an actual devil might conceivably glance at the fact that the river which runs near Hexham (on whose banks the battle was fought) is the Devil's Water, but more fundamentally it testifies both to the ambiguity of Dunstan's reputation and to the play's odd religious politics. On the one hand, there might seem to be a Protestant sensibility informing the moment when the coney-catcher rather belatedly asks the priest 'Brother, why do you not read to my father?' and the priest explains, 'Trulie my booke of exhortation is at my place of Exercise, and without it I can doe nothing: Gods peace bee with him' (sig. B3r). On the other hand, John the Precise shows that new priests are no better than the monks they replaced, and during the Beyond Shakespeare project's exploration of the play Renaissance scholar Steve Longstaffe observed 'The guy who relieves the poor – he sounds like a monastery or something like that – he reminds me of things people said after the Reformation, "Who's going to relieve the poor?"'.[18]

Above all, however, *A Knack to Know a Knave* is in dialogue with *Doctor Faustus*. Arthur Freeman calls *A Knack to Know a Knave* 'an extremely allusive play'[19] and Tom Rutter suggests that *Friar Bacon and Friar Bungay* may have been an influence as well as *Doctor Faustus*,[20] but *Doctor Faustus* is the principal and I think the most significant influence. The climax of Marlowe's play is directly echoed when the bailiff of Hexham is carried to Hell by the devil:

> Ah see my sonnes, where death, pall Death appeares,
> To summon me before a fearfull Iudge:
> Me thiuks reuenge stands with an yron whip,
> And cries repent, or I will punish thee:
> My heart is hardened, I cannot repent.
> Ah hark, me thinkes the Iudge doth giue my doome,
> And I am damn'd to euer burning fyre:
> Soule, be thou safe, and bodie flie to hell.
> *He dyeth.*
> *Enter Deuil, and carie him away.*
> (sig. B3r)

'My heart's so hardened I cannot repent' is also the lament of Faustus,[21] and he too is carried off bodily by devils who tear him from limb from limb, at least in the 1616 text. However, that may or may not represent the play which the author of *A Knack to Know a Knave* would have seen in the theatre; in the 1604 text, the emphasis is not on Faustus' body but on his soul, and I think that difference helps us to see what is really frightening about *Doctor Faustus*. I have argued that *Thorney Abbey* implies that a place can have sacred power, and I'll repeat that claim for the two texts I'll discuss in subsequent chapters; *Doctor Faustus* proposes that Hell is everywhere and nowhere is safe from it. This is a subject on which *A Knack to Know a Knave* is agnostic. It takes us to Hexham but tantalisingly says nothing at all about its famous abbey, which is the centrepiece of the town and visible from afar (let alone that it was the burial site of Aelfwald, canonised king of Northumbria); it shows us King Edgar but offers no hint of the thing for which he was principally known, the reintroduction of Benedictine monasticism; it shows us Dunstan but turns him into a conjurer of the devil rather than an abbot or an archbishop. It does, however, show us an England in which mediaeval traditions of hospitality are declining and in which Honesty finds small welcome, and perhaps in so doing it invites us to draw our own conclusions.

Notes

1 Hanspeter Born, 'Why Greene was Angry at Shakespeare', *Medieval & Renaissance Drama in England* 25 (2012), pp. 133–723.
2 Paul H. Kocher, 'The English Faust Book and the Date of Marlowe's Faustus', *Modern Language Notes* 55. 2 (February, 1940), pp. 95–101, pp. 96–97.
3 Alexandra Walsham, *The Reformation of the Landscape: Religion, Identity, and Memory in Early Modern Britain and Ireland* (Oxford: Oxford University Press, 2011), p. 490.
4 Mercedes Salvador-Bello, 'The Edgar Panegyrics in the *Anglo-Saxon Chronicle*', in *Edgar, King of the English 959–975: New Interpretations*, edited by Donald Scragg (Woodbridge: The Boydell Press, 2008), pp. 252–272, p. 255 n. 9.
5 Simon Keynes, 'Edgar, *rex admirabilis*', in *Edgar, King of the English 959–975: New Interpretations*, edited by Donald Scragg (Woodbridge: The Boydell Press, 2008), pp. 3–58, p. 57.
6 Lawrence Manley and Sally Beth Maclean, *Lord Strange's Men and Their Plays* (New Haven: Yale University Press, 2014), p. 276.
7 Peter Rex, *Edgar, King of the English 959–75* (Stroud: Tempus, 2007), pp. 10 and 42.
8 Rex, *Edgar, King of the English 959–75*, pp. 44 and 75.
9 Rex, *Edgar, King of the English 959–75*, pp. 106 and 121.
10 Donna Hamilton, 'Catholic Use of Anglo-Saxon Precedents, 1565–1625', *Recusant History* 26.4 (October 2003), pp. 537–55, pp. 543 and 546–7.
11 Anonymous, *A most pleasant and merie nevv comedie, intituled, A knacke to knowe a knaue Newlie set foorth, as it hath sundrie tymes bene played by Ed. Allen and his companie. VVith Kemps applauded merrimentes of the men of Goteham, in receiuing the King into Goteham* (London: Richard Jones, 1594), sig. A2r.
12 https://lostplays.folger.edu/Battle_of_Hexham.
13 *Laws, etc.; At the Parliament begunne and holden at Westminster [8 May–30 June 1572]* (London: Richard Jugge, 1572), EEBO image 23.
14 Todd Andrew Borlik, *Shakespeare Beyond the Green World: Drama and Ecopolitics in Jacobean Britain*. Oxford: Oxford University Press, 2023), p. 16.
15 Rex, *Edgar, King of the English 959–75*, p. 156.
16 Tom Rutter, *Shakespeare and the Admiral's Men: Reading Across Repertories on the London Stage, 1594–1600* (Cambridge: Cambridge University Press, 2017), p. 75.
17 Lawrence Manley and Sally Beth Maclean, *Lord Strange's Men and Their Plays* (New Haven: Yale University Press, 2014), p. 228.
18 *A Knack to Know a Knave*, first look, part 1 (Beyond Shakespeare Exploring Sessions) https://www.youtube.com/watch?v=X1y2uODgh8U.
19 Arthur Freeman, 'Two Notes on *A Knack to Know a Knave*', *Notes and Queries* 207 (1962), pp. 326–7, p. 326.
20 Tom Rutter, *Shakespeare and the Admiral's Men: Reading Across Repertories on the London Stage, 1594–1600* (Cambridge: Cambridge University Press, 2017), p. 74.
21 Christopher Marlowe, *Doctor Faustus*, 1604 text, in *Christopher Marlowe: The Complete Plays*, edited by Mark Thornton Burnett (London: J. M. Dent, 1999), 2.3.18.

Chapter 3

A SHOEMAKER A GENTLEMAN

William Rowley's *A Shoemaker a Gentleman* was published in 1638, but had clearly been written some time before: the prefatory matter declares that 'as Plaies were then, some twenty yeares agone, it was in the fashion',[1] which would give a date of c. 1618 if taken literally, and Trudi L. Darby argues that this is indeed the likeliest time for it to have been composed.[2] The title suggests that its main agenda is to tell the story of Saints Crispin and Crispian, but it also has a lot of other things to do: though the Crispin and Crispian scenes take place mainly in Faversham, we also visit St Winifred's Well and St Albans, and whereas both Crispin and Crispian, unusually for saints, live happily ever after, we also meet the martyrs St Hugh, St Winifred, St Alban and St Amphiabel (more usually called St Amphibalus, though that, in fact, means 'cloak' and derives from a story about someone who gave St Alban a cloak to enable him to disguise himself). St Alban, England's first martyr, was also the possible or certain subject of two lost plays, *Warlamchester* and James Shirley's *The Tragedy of St Albans*, either or both of which might have described his martyrdom, and St Albans was a suggestive location because it had recently been the scene of a power struggle between civic and religious authorities. In his biography of Bess of Hardwick, Wyn Derbyshire observes of St Albans that 'as the sixteenth century dawned, the Abbey began to suffer a decline, as exemplified by the fact that St Albans town began to break free of the Abbey's dominance, with the townsfolk gaining control of important civic posts, such as those of the town bailiff and the clerk of the market, offices which had previously been at the disposal of the Abbot'[3]; Derbyshire argues that this made the abbey easy prey for Bess's second husband William Cavendish and the other commissioners implementing the dissolution.

A Shoemaker a Gentleman opens with King Allured (a phonetic spelling of Alfred, though the figure in the play has little in common with the historical ninth-century Alfred) brought in wounded and on the point of death, accompanied by the Queen and their sons Eldred and Offa (two names which further destabilise our sense of time and place, since Offa was an eighth-century king of Mercia and Eadred a tenth-century king of the English). They wish to stay and guard him, but Alfred exhorts them to save themselves and leave him to die; the Queen significantly accuses him of 'dispaire' (sig. B1r) but he says there is no choice but to accept that as a result of the defeat just suffered,

> Those bloody Persecutors *Maximinus,* and *Dioclesian,*
> Display their by neckt Eagle over Brittaine.
> (sig. B1v)

He dies and his son Eldred decides

> Brother, it shall be thus; some poore Souldier slaine in the
> Battaile will we change habits with: so it may be thought
> That wee are slaine, and stay the bloody Inquisition.
> (sig. B2r)

We are, therefore, in either the eighth, ninth or tenth centuries, but there are Romans in Britain, the Inquisition is a force to be feared, and the Queen seems to have an early modern understanding of despair as a sin. However, at least we are definitely in England (except when we're not) so we can be reasonably confident that what is at stake are the religious and cultural politics of a post-Reformation society in which there is a clear nostalgia for saints as significant figures for feast days and guilds but a reluctance to associate them too closely with doctrinal or theological issues (though the play is not averse to using them as symbols of resistance to the abuse of secular power).

Despite the Queen's wish to remain with her dying husband, the Welsh prince Hugh promises to escort her to safety in North Wales where his father reigns over Powys, though a second Welsh prince, Amphiabel, warns Hugh that he has heard from Winifred, daughter and heir of the late king Dunwallo, that the Romans have invaded there too and are martyring Christians; Winifred herself is still safe but

> Hath left off State, forsaken Royalty,
> And keepes a Court so solitary, as it seemes
> More like a Cloyster, then a Royall Pallace.
> (sig. B2v)

The queen decides to stay with the body of Allured and the victorious Maximilian and Dioclesian enter, congratulating themselves but also commending the still-pagan Alban, whom they appoint as steward of Great Britain and Baron of Verulam, where he is to be based in order to persecute

Christians in conjunction with his colleague Bassianus. Discovering the queen, Maximilian threatens to prostitute her to a slave, to which she replies 'And such an other may thy Daughter have' (sig. B3v), presumably gesturing at Leodice, who will be an important character in the play. In fact, Maximilian sends the queen to Rochester Castle, while the two emperors themselves depart for France and Leodice is to 'keep her court at *Canterbury*' (sig. B4r).

The scene then switches to a shoemaker's shop in Faversham, where we meet the shoemaker himself, his wife Sisly, and his apprentice Barnaby, whom the shoemaker jovially promises to feed on beef 'As good as the Major of *Feversham* cuts on's Trencher' (sig. B4v). These people are secret Christians, though the apprentice shoemaker Barnaby jokes,

> I am afraide there will be too many Christians sir,
> Because many use to goe a Pilgrimage Bare-foot;
> And that's an ill wind for our profit.
> (sig. B4v)

The fleeing princes Eldred and Offa, now disguised and calling themselves Crispinus and Crispianus, enter the shop as one of the younger boys starts to sing and are instantly captivated by the cheerful atmosphere, with Eldred declaring,

> Brother, heer's a life to mocke at state, and staine her surly
> Greatnesse: who would venture to walke upon the Icy path
> Of Royalty, that here might find a footing so secure:
> Heer's harmony indeed, a fearelesse sport,
> A joy our young yeares seld, has at Court.
> (sig. B4v)

Offa agrees and they offer themselves as apprentices. The shoemaker has just accepted this proposal when the queen is brought past on her way to prison and spots her sons. It is too dangerous for either she or they to give any open sign of recognition, but the compassionate Sisly offers the queen a stool and she seizes the opportunity to bless the boys surreptitiously. After she has been taken away, Sisly comments 'The world treads not upright, methinkes / It had neede of a good workeman to mend it' (sig. C2r), suggesting that the interactions between the shoemaker's household and all surviving members of the royal family are not simply a part of the story but that they, along with Eldred's praise of the middle-class state, offer implicit but pointed comment on the ways that rulers should act.

The scene then shifts again to Wales. This is an unusual manoeuvre because early mediaeval Wales was often understood as being automatically opposed to early mediaeval England: Alexandra Walsham notes that 'According to a memorandum written by Lord Burghley, "harpers and Crowthers" sung "songes of the doeinges of theire Auncestors namelie of theire warrs againste the kinges of this realme and the English nacion"'.[4] *A Shoemaker a Gentleman*, however, features saints from both countries and draws no significant distinction between them since both the Welsh and the English saints are opposed not to each other but to Rome. Monika Fludernik argues that 'The blending of a saint's legend with a historical tale of patriotic resistance to Roman occupation is highly innovative',[5] and perhaps it is radical politically as well as narratively, since it decouples Catholicism from Roman oppression. Moreover, even though the name of one prince, Offa, evokes the most famous boundary between England and Wales a very different effect is achieved when Alban addresses Amphiabel as 'Prince of *Wales*' (sig. D2v), which not only establishes him as a cross-over figure who is both a territorial magnate and a spiritual leader but also points up the fact that since the late thirteenth century the Prince of Wales had been designated successor to the King of England.

We first meet Winifred wearing a black veil and accompanied by the two Welsh princes Amphiabel and Hugh, whom the stage direction cheerfully if prematurely identifies as 'Saint Hugh' (sig. C2v), a title which he immediately belies by importuning Winifred to marry him. Winifred promises him a decision in three months, but reveals after he has left that Amphiabel has converted her to a life of chastity, although Amphiabel himself reminds her that wedlock is not a sin and that he wants her to be a Christian rather than necessarily a virgin, an important clarification since Catholicism was often accused of fetishing virginity.

However, Winifred says she has sworn an oath which has been confirmed by a miracle:

> See you this spring, here a pretty streame begins his head,
> So late it was a parching drought had ceas'd our verdant grasse,
> Here did I sit in Contemplation, lifting to Heaven my Orisons
> For present succour, but swifter then my thought,
> All Potent Heaven a Miracle had wrought:
> That Barren seeming Ground brought forth a Spring
> Of such sweet waters, as it had not beene curst I'th' old worlds
> Deluge, I caus'd it then thus to be digg'd and fram'd
> By hand of men, and comming still to see it as before,
> A Heavenly shape appear'd, and blest it more;

> Gave it that power as heaven had so assign'd,
> To cure diseases, helpe the lame and blind:
> For which poore people their poore thanks to tell,
> Calls as I would not, *Winifreds* Well.
> (sig. C3v)

Amphiabel is impressed, and even more so when an angel appears out of the well, pronounces it blessed, and descends into it again. As a result of this encounter, Amphiabel immediately decides to go to Verulam and seek to persuade Alban, whom he describes as 'Our friend and fellow Knight' (sig. C4r), to stop persecuting Christians.

The second act begins with Leodice telling her nurse that one of her new shoes hurts, which turns out to be an excuse for recalling Crispinus, who made it and to whom she has taken a fancy. The nurse says Crispinus needs to know the length of her foot and goes to call him; left alone, Leodice muses,

> The length of my foot, a pretty figure
> If he be a good Anatomist, he may by one quantity
> Guesse at another, and in the end take the whole bodies length
> (sig. D1r)

This bawdy by-play seems to be in stark contrast to Winifred's commitment to chastity, but in keeping with its wariness about overvaluing virginity, the play does not in any sense condemn Leodice, who is mainly presented as the instrument by which Crispinus regains the position of power to which he was born. Meanwhile Amphiabel, disguised as a hermit, has converted Alban to Christianity. When Maximinus returns, he is surprised to find that Alban is not killing anyone and demands 'why art not wading in a / Sreame of blood? true *Romans* to swim in such a floud' (sig. D3r), to which Alban replies 'But I am an English man' (sig. D3r). When Maximinus insists 'Yet substitute to *Rome*' (sig. D3r) he replies simply 'Not' (sig. D3r); this exchange crudely but effectively evokes the long and difficult history of debates about the extent of English Catholics' allegiance to the Pope, dating back to Henry VIII's introduction of the concept of *praemunire* in the 1530s, peaking when Pius V excommunicated Elizabeth I in 1570, and rumbling on ever since.

Maximinus immediately deduces that Alban must have been talking to Amphiabel, for whom he orders a search to be made; however, Alban explains that he has sent Amphiabel to safety while he himself has remained to face martyrdom to atone for his previous persecution of Christians. Maximinus orders Alban to be tortured and dispatches Bassianus to Wales in search of Winifred and 'that seminary Knight *Amphiabell*' (sig. D3v), vowing

> Bloud is the theame we treate in *Roman* hand,
> Weele write the comment large o're all the Land.
> (sig. D4r)

The term 'seminary knight' unmistakably invites us to transpose an apparently long-dead conflict into urgently modern terms and apply it directly to the contemporary situation, just as 'This dramatic version of the romance of Crispin and Crispianus creates a strong link between the common populations of ancient Britain and that of contemporary audiences in Jacobean England'.[6] Act Two concludes with Leodice persuading Crispinus to admit that he loves her, upon which he reveals his identity as Offa and they prepare to marry.

Act Three opens with Hugh returning at the end of the three-month waiting period enjoined on him to solicit Winifred again. She refuses him, but she and Amphiabel are promptly surprised by the Romans. One Roman, Lutius, is blinded when he mockingly rubs water from the well onto his eyes; lashing out, he wounds the Roman commander Bassianus, upon which Winifred miraculously restores his sight, but Bassianus nevertheless orders both her and Amphiabel to be taken to Verulam to witness the torture of Alban. This sight-related miracle echoes traditional stories about the virtues of St Winifred's Well: Alexandra Walsham describes how 'Anecdotes about the supernatural punishment of the scoffing Elizabethan Protestant William Shone, who maliciously profaned the water of Holywell with his muddy boots, had a long life in accounts of the shrine. A similar lesson was enshrined in the tale of Lowry Davies, who went to the well "rather out of pastime then devotion" and spoke out irreligiously against its healing waters, only to find herself struck suddenly "stark blind"';[7] the alleged blinding of Lowry Davies occurred in 1617, just around the time when *A Shoemaker a Gentleman* was probably being written.

Meanwhile, back in Faversham, the Roman recruiter Rutullus visits the shoemaker to pressgang one of his apprentices and Crispianus volunteers, to be immediately replaced as apprentice by Hugh, who has followed the captured Winifred. The scene then shifts to France where Dioclesian is confronting Huldrick, King of the Goths, and Roderick, King of the Vandals, who threaten to turn their attentions to Rome itself once they have conquered France but are routed by a charge led by Crispianus, who personally rescues Dioclesian from Roderick and Huldrick in turn and also retrieves a captured Eagle.

Act Four opens on Crispinus and a pregnant Leodice as the inhabitants of Faversham turn out *en masse* to witness the martyrdoms of Amphiabel, Winifred and Alban, leading Crispinus to comment,

> Misery of times when Kings doe kill,
> Not arm'd by Law to doe it, but by will.
> (sig. G4r)

Crispinus now confesses both his identity and his marriage to the shoemaker and his wife, who offer to shelter Leodice if he will carry her off after having first caused a distraction by lighting the beacons on the cliffs of Dover; however, they cannot help Hugh, who has revealed his identity so he may die alongside Winifred. She chooses to bleed to death and he is forced to drink the blood, which has been collected in a cup and then had poison added to it, an echo of *Hamlet* which is confirmed when Hugh dies saying,

> Angels shall clap their wings to ring my knell,
> And bid me welcome to the land of rest
> (sig. J2v)

The shoemakers bury his body and agree that their tools will henceforth always be known as St Hugh's Bones.

Act Five begins with some country people in an uproar about the tree which Crispinus has set on fire to make people think the beacons have been lit and so cover Leodice's escape. The Roman camp is alarmed by the apparent lighting of the beacons, but the returning Crispianus is able to reassure them that he has not sighted any enemies and is reunited with Crispinus, who announces the birth of a boy. Crispianus is offered the reward of his choice for his valour in rescuing Dioclesian and requests the release of his mother, at the same time revealing his identity as Eldred. Maximinus assents to this and also tries to offer him the hand of Leodice, but she arrives with Crispinus and their baby and Maximinus agrees to accept their marriage. Finally, the shoemakers beg that 25 October may always be kept as a holiday and Crispinus declares that

> A Church then, and a beauteous Monastery
> On *Holmhurst*-Hill, where *Albon* lost his head,
> *Offa* shall build; which Ile St. *Albons* name,
> In honour of our first English Martyrs fame.
> (sig. J4v)

Maximinus responds,

> Build what Religious Monuments you please,
> Be true to *Rome*, none shall disturbe your peace.
> (sig. J4v)

He thus offers religious tolerance on condition of civil obedience, an implicit endorsement of the longstanding insistence by many early modern English and Welsh Catholics that they were not the fifth column of the Pope but were perfectly well able to continue being good subjects of the Crown while still practising their faith.

The Printer's address to practitioners of 'the Gentle Craft', as shoemaking was often termed, declares that

> it is well knowne to you (Gentlemen Cordwiners) that every yeare you doe celebrate the Feast of *Crispine*, & *Crispianus*, not in a meane and ordinary way, but with a great deale of Ceremony, keeping it as an Holyday, feasting and entertaining your friends and neighbours.
> (sigs A3r-v)

This is an obvious glance at *Henry V*, where the Battle of Agincourt is 'Fought on the day of Crispin Crispian' and the king prophesies that

> He that shall see this day and live old age
> Will yearly on the vigil feast his neighbours,
> And say 'Tomorrow is Saint Crispian.'[8]

But Henry's prophecy had not aged well, because as Jonathan Baldo reminds us, there was no annual commemoration of Agincourt and celebration of St Crispin's Day would have been viewed as suspect in post-Reformation England;[9] although, as Donna Hamilton notes, Thomas Stapleton, who translated Bede, included a dedication to the queen in which he 'praised [Henry V] for having put down the rebellion of John Oldcastle and the heresy of John Wickliffe',[10] Henry's devotion to SS Crispin and Crispian now verged on looking heretical in its own right. St Winifred and St Alban were similarly tainted, all the more so because the college at Valladolid, which was founded by Robert Persons, was named the College of St Alban and the supposedly miraculous pilgrimage site of St Winifred's Well not only continued to figure prominently in the popular consciousness long after the Reformation but was directly associated with sedition:[11] Phebe Jensen notes that 'Bodleian manuscript Eng.poet.b.5, transcribed in the mid-1650s and associated with the household of the Catholic yeoman Thomas Fairfax of Warwickshire, contains thirty-two poems by Robert Southwell, two poems on Campion [...] [and] two poems to St. Winifred',[12] coupling the saint with the executed Jesuit Edmund Campion, and the Gunpowder plotters made a pilgrimage to St Winifred's Well shortly before the plot itself. Nevertheless, the Prologue to *A Shoemaker a Gentleman* boldly declares 'it is a Play that is often Acted; and when others fade and are out of date, yet this doth endure tò the Last' (sig. A3v), punning on the cobbler's last but also defiantly asserting the continuing interest of this provocative story about saints.

A Shoemaker a Gentleman offers sad endings for some of its characters but happy endings for others (albeit from a Christian perspective martyrdom is also a happy ending). Gina M. Di Salvo notes that this is in line with other Jacobean examples of allowing Crispin and Crispian to survive and flourish instead of having them become martyrs: she observes that 'On Friday, 20 August 1613 the Cordwainers of Wells presented a pageant of SS Crispin and Crispianus to entertain Anna of Denmark, the wife of James I' and that 'The Cordwainers' own records document the stage properties and costumes in the guild's possession and that a cast of four actors played the two saints, Lady Ursula, and the nurse to the child of the lady'.[13] (This pageant in turn built on Thomas Deloney's *The Gentle Craft*.) However, Di Salvo suggests that both Deloney and the devisers of the cordwainers' pageant were affected by considerations of time: she suggests that Ursula was chosen because 'Ursula's feast day falls on 21 October and is the liturgical observation that immediately precedes the feast of Crispin and Crispianus on 25 October'.[14] Alison A. Chapman develops this idea even further when she argues that *A Shoemaker a Gentleman* belongs to a group of plays whose primary concern is dates: 'Typically, texts that feature these sole/soul menders also raise questions of festal observance, most often by showing the shoemakers creating, or attempting to create, new holy days'.[15] (In Thomas Dekker's *The Shoemaker's Holiday*, Firk says 'we'll make Shrove Tuesday Saint George's Day for you'.[16])

By contrast, it is axiomatic in *A Shoemaker A Gentleman* that power is invested in place. Maximinus orders that the shrine at St Winifred's Well should be destroyed:

> lay desolate the confines of that superstitious
> Virgin, that with her sorcerous devotion works miracles,
> By which she drawes Christians, faster than we can kill 'em.
> (sig. D3v)

However Winifred informs the Romans that to do this is beyond their power:

> […] tyrant, this place is hallowed; doe not awake
> the thunder, if it strike, the boult will fall downe
> Perpendicular, and strike thee under mercy.
> (sig. E4r)

She is not martyred until after she has been removed from the well and taken to Verulamium as if the well had been sustaining and protecting her. Her journey there connects the play's two apparently disparate locations of North Wales and St Albans, but in fact, there was already a link between them in that both were associated with sacred waters: Alexandra Walsham observes that 'a well at St Albans was the site where England's first martyr had lost his head'.[17] She also notes that

> Holywell […] became the jewel in the Crown of the Welsh Catholic revival. Even in the sixteenth century the spring and chapel had been the headquarters of the Catholic mission to the region, and by the mid-seventeenth, served by the Jesuits and seculars from the two inns in the town […] it had wholly reclaimed its reputation as a destination of pious pilgrims from much further afield. Its popularity was fostered by Falconer's new edition of the life of St Winefride.[18]

Around the time when *A Shoemaker A Gentleman* was probably written, 'the audacity of the annual gatherings of pilgrims at Holywell on St Winefride's feast day was palpable. In November 1620, when Bishop Lewis Bayly of Bangor went to the spring in person to arrest patrons congregated there, the local populace rose up against him, "handled him roughly and then threw him into a ditch"'.[19] Partly the well was protected by its association with the Tudors – the chapel which covered it had been built by Henry VII's mother Margaret Beaufort – but mainly it could not be threatened because it was simply too beloved, not only by the local populace but also as one of the few remaining pilgrimage sites in the British Isles. In *A Shoemaker a Gentleman*, we hear a clear echo of that love along with a plea for acceptance that English and Welsh Catholics are not agents of Rome, and we are taken too to Faversham, reminding us that in *Arden of Faversham* all attempts to murder Arden fail until the killers attack him in his own home, which had once been the gatehouse of Faversham Abbey. Arden's back garden seems to remember its former sacred status when a sudden snowfall is stained with his blood and makes his killers' tracks visible; in *A Shoemaker a Gentleman* too, places retain the power they once had.

Notes

1 William Rowley, *A Shoo-maker a Gentleman* (London: John Okes for John Cowper, 1638), sig. A4r.
2 Trudi L. Darby, 'The Date of William Rowley's *A Shoemaker, A Gentleman*', *Notes and Queries* 53.1 (2006), pp. 83–4.
3 Wyn Derbyshire, *Bess of Hardwick: An Elizabethan Tycoon* (London: Spiramus Press, 2022), p. 19.
4 Alexandra Walsham, *The Reformation of the Landscape: Religion, Identity, and Memory in Early Modern Britain and Ireland* (Oxford: Oxford University Press, 2011), p. 203.
5 Monika Fludernik, 'Early modern dramatic martyrdom', in *Enacting the Bible in Medieval and Early Modern Drama*, edited by Eva von Contzen and Chanita Goodblatt (Manchester: Manchester University Press, 2020), pp. 192–210, p. 201.
6 Gina M. Di Salvo, 'Saints' Lives and Shoemakers' Holidays: *The Gentle Craft* and the Wells Cordwainers' Pageant of 1613', *Early Theatre* 19.2 (2016), pp. 119–138, p. 127.
7 Walsham, *The Reformation of the Landscape*, pp. 204 and 535.
8 William Shakespeare, *King Henry V*, edited by T. W. Craik (London: Routledge, 1995), 4.7.90 and 4.3.44–6.
9 Jonathan Baldo, 'Wars of Memory in *Henry V*', *Shakespeare Quarterly* 47.2 (summer 1996), pp. 132–59, p. 137.
10 Donna Hamilton, 'Catholic Use of Anglo-Saxon Precedents, 1565–1625', *Recusant History* 26.4 (October 2003), pp. 537–55, p. 538.
11 See Alison Shell, 'Divine Muses, Catholic Poets and Pilgrims to St Winifred's Well: Literary Communities in Francis Chetwinde's "New Hellicon" (1642)', in *Writing and Religion in England, 1558–1689: Studies in Community-Making and Cultural Memory*, edited by Roger D. Sell and Anthony W. Johnson (Burlington: Ashgate, 2009), pp. 273–88. Shell discusses Francis Chetwinde's 1642 poem 'The New Hellicon' and argues, 'In the mythological schema of the poem, St Winifred stands in for Mnemosyne, mother of the Muses and patroness of the fountain named after her, whose springs counteracted Lethe's waters of oblivion' (p. 288).
12 Phebe Jensen, *Religion and Revelry in Shakespeare's Festive World* (Cambridge: Cambridge University Press, 2008), p. 58.
13 Di Salvo, 'Saints' Lives and Shoemakers' Holidays', p. 119.
14 Di Salvo, 'Saints' Lives and Shoemakers' Holidays', p. 123.
15 Alison A. Chapman, 'Whose Saint Crispin's Day Is It Anyway?: Shoemaking, Holiday Making, and the Politics of Memory in Early Modern England', *Renaissance Quarterly* 54 (2001), pp. 1467–94, p. 1467.
16 Thomas Dekker, *The Shoemaker's Holiday*, in *Six Plays by Contemporaries of Shakespeare*, edited by C. B. Wheeler (Oxford: Oxford University Press, 1915), V.ii.87–8.
17 Walsham, *The Reformation of the Landscape*, p. 42.
18 Walsham, *The Reformation of the Landscape*, p. 196.
19 Walsham, *The Reformation of the Landscape*, p. 201.

Chapter 4

THE LOVESICK KING

At some point in the early seventeenth century, an otherwise unknown playwright called Anthony Brewer wrote a play called *The Lovesick King*, set nominally during the reign of King Canute although the subplot centres on a Newcastle merchant named Roger Thornton who lived during the fourteenth century.¹ Although it was not published until 1655, M. Hope Dodds argues that it was certainly written for one of James I's two visits to Newcastle in 1603 and 1617, since its main agenda is to showcase the splendours of Newcastle. Dodds thinks 1617 the likelier date, since there would not have been much time to prepare it in 1603 when James was in the city from 9 to 13 April on his way south after the death of Elizabeth;² however, I think the earlier date is the more probable because the play seems likely to have been commissioned by the local Catholic aristocrat John, Lord Lumley, whose home at Lumley Castle King James visited on 13 April 1603, when he saw portraits which included those of Lumley's first wife Jane Lumley, daughter of the Earl of Arundel, and her first cousin Lady Jane Grey.³ At some point in the early 1550s, Lady Jane Lumley translated Euripides' play *Iphigenia at Aulis* into English, becoming both his first English translator and the first known Englishwoman to write a play. Although her achievement has sometimes been scorned and her grasp of Greek derided, recent scholarship has provided new evidence for her competence and shown that her translation offers a powerful meditation on the fate of Lumley's cousin, Lady Jane Grey.

Jane Lumley's translation of *Iphigenia at Aulis* also introduces new implications and emphases not present in the original, including an interest in the concept of the commodity. Achilles reports that when he protested against the sacrifice of Iphigeneia, he was told that he was only saying that because he was in love with her, and 'I did preferre myne owne pleasure, aboue the co[m]modite of my countrie' (lines 1124–25), and later Iphigeneia herself tells her mother Clytemnestra that 'I was not borne for your sake onlie, but rather for the co[m]modite of my countrie' (lines 1185–87).⁴ Although it did not yet carry quite all of its modern connotations of capitalism and global trade, the word 'commodity' already meant a thing that could be bought; in *The Comedy of Errors*, Antipholus of Syracuse, walking through the streets of Ephesus, notes that 'some offer me commodities to buy' (4.3.6).[5] Iphigeneia implicitly recognises her own status as object, but the play also tacitly acknowledges the growing importance attached to objects and trade. So too does *The Lovesick King*, which also echoes the subtext of *Iphigenia in Aulis* in featuring a doomed princess who explicitly asserts her English identity.

Jane Lumley died in 1578, but she was not forgotten; her widower John, Lord Lumley erected a tomb for her in 1596 as well as showing King James her picture in 1603. John Lumley, whose autograph signature appears on the first leaf of the manuscript of his wife's *Iphigeneia*, was both a direct descendant of Roger Thornton (whose only child had transmitted his whole fortune to the Lumleys) and a coal-mining magnate, and much is made in the play of the importance of coal to Newcastle's prosperity. John Leland recorded that

> Roger Thornton was the richest merchant ever to dwell in Newcastle. He lived in the time of Edward IV, and built St Katharine's Chapel, the town hall, and an almshouse for poor men, which he sited next to Sandhill Gate within the town, a little below Newcastle Bridge and right on the bank of the Tyne. His daughter and heiress married into the Lumley family, and greatly increased their possessions [...] almost all [...] they own in Yorkshire and Northumberland, was inherited from Thornton.[6]

The fact that the Lumley family seat was at Chester-le-Street would have given Lumley a motive to commission a play extolling Newcastle and his almost fanatical interest in his own ancestry (of which he made such great play that James I is said to have remarked, 'I didna ken Adam's name was Lumley')[7] is likely to have been the prompt for the inclusion of Thornton. (Lumley also had an additional reason to be interested in history because his sister Barbara married the antiquarian Humphrey Lhuyd). When Randolfe's Wife asks of Thornton, 'Is hee not, think you Husband, one of those Players of Interludes that dwels at Newcastle, and conning of his Part' (sig. A4r) she might well refer to a local company hired by Lumley. It is also just possible that Lumley might already have been indirectly connected with a lost play about St Guthlac (who was closely associated with Crowland Abbey, one of the many Benedictine houses founded by King Edgar). Todd Andrew Borlik suggests that Guthlac may have been the eponymous hero of the lost play *Cutlack*; Matthew Steggle argues that it was in fact about the Danish king Guthlagh,[8] but Borlik's observation that an 'important manuscript of the Life of Guthlac belonged to the prominent recusant and book collector Lord Lumley'[9] is eye-catching in this context.

But if the family history and the idea for the play came from John Lumley, the prompt for using drama to speak of public events and influence opinion surely came from Jane Lumley. Canutus' sister Elgina, who falls in love with Alured, the future Alfred the Great, utters a resounding defence of her own identity when, pleading for Alured to be spared, she argues that 'If all the English perish, then must I, for I (now know) in England here was bred, although descended of the Danish blood, [the] King my Father, thirty years governed the one half of this famous Kingdom, where I, that time was born an English Princess' (sigs B2r-v). Brewer's Elgina, an unhistorical character with little to do in the plot except speak these lines and then sacrifice herself, might well glance at Lumley's Iphigeneia, who, in her capacity as stand-in for Lady Jane Grey, could also have made the claim that she too was born an English princess. Elgina, like Jane Lumley herself, will very soon die leaving no children behind her, but she has at least claimed a name, a voice, and a status, just as Jane Lumley's Iphigeneia claims her own identity as a daughter rather than having it foisted upon her.

Like *A Shoemaker a Gentleman*, *The Lovesick King* opens with an Anglo-Saxon king being defeated in battle. This time, it is King Etheldred of Wessex who is killed in an unsuccessful attempt to defend his capital city of Winchester from Danes led by King Canutus, leaving his brother Alured (better known as Alfred) as heir. (If *A Shoemaker a Gentleman* were set in a single time period, this would make it a prequel of sorts to *The Lovesick King*, but as we have seen, it is not, and indeed *The Lovesick King* isn't either.) The Danes are aided by the treacherous Osbert of Mercia, a character who is soon killed (by the victorious Canutus, who doesn't like traitors) but whose presence in the play may be connected to the Arden/Dudley struggle for power in Warwickshire, which had been waged partly through the attempt to appropriate (or fake) Anglo-Saxon ancestry. Glyn Parry and Cathryn Enis note that 'In the 1575 extravaganza at Kenilworth [when Robert Dudley entertained Elizabeth I] the Midlands had been recast as Mercia' and that 'in the early 1570s [...] [the herald Robert] Glover once again tried to link the Mercians with the earldom of Leicester': 'In Glover's notes, Edwin, never more than earl of Mercia, became duke of Mercia and earl of Leicester'.[10] Donna Hamilton suggestively comments that 'Saxon materials enlarge our understanding of Catholic interest in Anglo-Saxon roots, as exemplified by [...] the attention given to arms and genealogies by families like the Lumleys in the sixteenth century';[11] John Lumley was indeed obsessed with genealogy, so might well have been aware of the Arden/Dudley quarrel, which would make the play's reference to a villainous Duke of Mercia look distinctly pointed.

After being admitted by Osbert, the Danes sack both the city and St Swithin's Abbey (now Winchester Cathedral), crying 'Kill, kill' to make plain both their own wickedness and their resemblance to the Catholic killers of Huguenots during the St Bartholomew's Day Massacre.[12] The sense that the Danes are evil is also accentuated by the fact that, as Robert W. Dent points out, the story of *The Lovesick King* is 'an Anglicized version of a frequently dramatized story, that of Mahomet and the fair Irene at the fall of Constantinople',[13] which implicitly connects Canutus to the Ottoman Turks, and Alured refers to 'the usurped Temples of Canutus' (sig. G1v), again associating him with non-Christian worship. Canutus is also blasphemous and hubristic: as far as he is concerned, it is fine to kill all the English because 'The vanquish'd are but men, the Victors, gods' (sig. A3v).

The English disperse, with Duke Edmund flying to Thetford and Alured to Scotland to seek help from King Donald, while the scene shifts to the interior of the abbey at Winchester, where the nuns, led by the beautiful Cartesmunda, are clustering around the altar and hoping not to be raped. Canutus falls in love at first sight with Cartesmunda and has her sent to his tent, where she soon agrees to accept his love. (She obviously hasn't a lot of choice, but she does not seem reluctant.) Canutus' sister Elgina also falls in love at first sight with the captured Alured, disguised as Eldred; she saves him from execution and persuades her suitor Erkinwald to employ him as a servant, but the jealous Erkinwald soon detects her love for him and tries to kill Alured, only for Elgina to step between them and die. Alured avenges her by killing Erkinwald and then takes advantage of the fact that Canutus can think only of Cartesmunda to escape and raise an army, with such success that soon the only city still held by the Danes is York; when that too is taken, Canutus' lords try to reason with him and one, Huldrick, manages to kill Cartesmunda, although he dies himself. (Both Eldred and Huldrick are names also found in *A Shoemaker a Gentleman*; I think the influence must be from Brewer to Rowley, but that is only conjecture, and perhaps there is a third source or intertext of which I'm not aware.) As a result, Canutus comes to himself and begins to exert his authority again. Ironically although extradiegetically, he would live to be buried in Winchester, which Nicole Marafioti calls 'a location which posthumously confirmed his legitimacy [...] and placed his remains on par with those of earlier West Saxon kings' since Winchester Old Minster had been 'a favoured mausoleum of the West Saxon dynasty';[14] it was also, of course, the very church he despoils at the beginning of the play.

Act Two of the play takes us not only to another place but another time because the fourteenth-century Newcastle merchant Thornton lived five hundred years after Alfred and four hundred after Canute. When we first meet him, Thornton is a poor pedlar, but a witch has assured him that if he can get himself taken on as a servant in Newcastle, he will make his fortune.

Confident that he is destined to become the richest subject in the land, he vows to 'build some famous Monument' (sig. B3v) and later apostrophises the city of Newcastle,

> To grace thy fame, Ile beautifie thy ground,
> And build a wall that shall imbrace thee round.
> (sig. D3v)

Apparently, there will be 'A hundred fourscore Towers to grace the Walls' (sig. E3r), which will be a 100 feet high and 12 feet broad. John Leland did indeed say of Newcastle that 'the strength and magnificens of the waulling of this town far passeth al the waulles of the cities of England, and most of the townes of Europe',[15] but the building of its walls is usually credited to William Rufus, looking to consolidate his grip on the area after his father's Harrying of the North in 1069–70: in Harding's *Chronicle*, we are told that William Rufus 'buylded the Newcastell upon Tyne The Scottes to gaynstande'. Some parts of the walls seem to predate this and indeed to include elements of Roman fortification, but the play is probably right in ascribing the West Gate, which was pulled down in 1811, to Thornton.

Thornton also resolves that 'Amidst these poor indeavors of my love, my careful Master must not be forgot, whose Heir I am become, and for his sake, I will reedifie Alhallows Church, where in the peaceful bed of death he sleeps, and build a Tomb for him cut out in Touchstone, which in our Persian Voyage was return'd, from whence my golden Mineral arriv'd' (sig. F1v). The importance of minerals and fossil fuels to Newcastle's economy is confirmed when Thornton's old acquaintance Grim the Collier explains that he has heard that 'there are a new sort of Colliers crept up neer London, at a place call'd Croydon, that have found out a way by scorching of wood to make Charcoals, and 'tis to be fear'd this may hinder our Traffick' (sig. C3v); however, Grim (a figure who also has an intertextual relationship with *Thorney Abbey*, as seen in the first chapter) boasts that 'I dare undertake with my seven hundred Colliers in six days, under ground, to march to London, they shall dig their way themselves too' (sig. F2v). It is Grim and his colliers who eventually take Canutus prisoner, though Alured spares Canutus' life for Elgina's sake; their privileges are consequently confirmed and Grim can say 'Then stand thy ground, old Coal of Newcastle, and a fig for Croyden' (sig. G1r).

The Lovesick King's praise of Newcastle might well have been prompted partly by a reaction against James I's briefly entertained proposal to set up his capital at York in imitation of Constantine,[16] who had been proclaimed emperor there. *The Lovesick King* implicitly opposes this idea by going out of its way to present York as both tainted by its long association with the Danes and also dangerously vulnerable to attack: despite the strength of its Roman walls, York falls to the Scots, who threaten to level it with the earth unless the Danes yield the city (sig. E4r). (It might also have been remembered that although the historical Canute's father Sveyn Forkbeard had been interred first in York, his body was disinterred after a year and translated to Roskilde, presumably on the grounds that it would be safer there.)

Like *Thorney Abbey*, *The Lovesick King* evokes the story that Shakespeare tells in *Macbeth*, although it does so primarily in order to register its own difference from it. *The Lovesick King* features a king of Scots called Donald and another Scot called Malcolm, but these apparent nods to the Macbeth story are counteracted by the fact that it is the Scots who help civilise England rather than *vice versa*, an obvious compliment to King James. The Scots help Alured march as far as York, which they threaten with destruction if it does not yield, but they are very pointedly dissociated from the pillage and devastation which historical cross-Border raids traditionally entailed, as we see when Alured says,

> I came now with my best Hors-manship from the Scotch Army, whose Royal King in Neighbor amity, is arm'd in my just cause, has past the Tweed with prosperous forrage through Northumberland, all Holds and Castles taken by the Danes restore themselves to his subjection in our behalf.
> (sig. F2r)

These are no Border Reivers or marauding half-savages but well-mannered and well-behaved troops who 'forage' prosperously rather than despoil, do not appear to have destroyed any property, and promptly pass over to English hands any cities they take. It seems only fitting that Alured at the close of the play should repay their help by gifting them some of England:

> Great King of Scotland, we are yet a debtor to your kind love, which thus we 'gin to pay, all those our Northern borders bounding on Cumberland, from Tine to Tweed, we add unto your Crown, so 'twas fore-promised, and 'tis now perform'd; Most fit it is that we be ever lovers; The Sea that binds us in one Continent,
> Doth teach us to imbrace two hearts in one,
> To strengthen both 'gainst all invasion.
> (sig. G2r)

This, presumably, is how King Duncan in *Macbeth* came to be in a position to name his elder son Prince of Cumberland.

This civilising of the Scots does not, however, quite disguise the fact that *Macbeth* tells a story about Northumbria as well as about Scotland. A website on the history of Viking Northumbria offers a slightly unexpected perspective on the events of Shakespeare's play:

> In 1054 Siward, the Earl of Northumbria, defeated the Scots under King Macbeth and Siward's nephew Malcolm Canmore was appointed Lord of Strathclyde and the Lothians. It was an attempt to bring the Scottish lowlands once more under Northumbrian control.

Macbeth certainly does not privilege such a perspective on events, but it does allow for it, reminding the audience both of Siward's status as earl of Northumberland and the fact that Malcolm is his nephew. Malcolm assures Macduff that even before he arrived, 'Old Seyward with ten thousand warlike men / Already at a point, was setting forth',[17] making it quite clear that the invasion of Scotland is a specifically Northumbrian rather than more generally English enterprise, and later Malcolm addresses Siward as 'worthy uncle' (5.6.2). It is also suggestive that Malcolm should close the play by saying to his followers, 'Henceforth be earls, the first that ever Scotland / In such an honour named' (5.7.92–3). Scotland may not have had earls as such but it had had jarls, such as Macbeth's cousin Thorfinn Sigurdsson who ruled not only Orkney but Caithness, and the climate of philological enquiry in the early seventeenth century would not have made it hard to perceive that the two words were cognate. When Malcolm converts his thanes to earls, he borrows the title of his Northumbrian uncle and extends it to Scotland, and by refusing to acknowledge the existence of jarls, he again implicitly dissociates Northumbria from any tainting element of Danishness. *The Lovesick King* may show the English having to be helped by the Scots, but alluding to *Macbeth* allows it to remind audiences that there have also been occasions when the Scots have had to be helped by the English, and specifically by Northumbria.

Hamlet too is a presence in *The Lovesick King*, occurring in the subplot concerning the hasty remarriage of Randolfe's widowed sister. When Randolfe first suggests to her that she could now marry the wealthy Thornton, she demurs, 'Hey, ho, Hee's a very honest man truly, and had my husband dyed but two months ago, I might ha' thought on't' (sig. E3r). After a little persuasion, however, she consents to marry him the same day; this looks pointed, as does the inclusion of a character with the name Osric. Echoes of *Hamlet* work to connect the inhabitants of Newcastle to the Danes and confirm the sense that there is contact between the two ostensibly disparate plots of *The Lovesick King*; moreover, *Hamlet* too is interested in walls and battlements, and understanding *The Lovesick King* as in dialogue with *Hamlet* helps us see things not only about Brewer's play but also about Shakespeare's. At an early stage of *The Lovesick King*, Osbert reminds Canutus that 'an hundred thirty years the English Kings have paid just tribute to the conquering Danes' (sig. A3r). That *Hamlet* is explicitly set during this period is signalled by the fact that Claudius dispatches him to England 'for the demand of our neglected tribute',[18] and also when we are told that the country he is expected to visit is one whose 'cicatrice looks raw and red / After the Danish sword' (IV.iv.63–4). Like *The Lovesick King*, too, *Hamlet* is notably interested in underground activity: the Ghost is a 'mole' who works fast in the earth (I.iv.170), and Hamlet reflects that

> 'tis the sport to have the enginer
> Hoist with his own petard, and't shall go hard
> But I will delve one yard below their mines
> And blow them at the moon.
> (III.iv.208–11)

As the Arden 2 edition notes, 'a *petard* was an explosive device, recently invented, for breaking through gates, walls, etc.', so this is a passage which has in mind exactly the kind of warfate which the walls of Newcastle were able to withstand.

For *The Lovesick King* to point to *Hamlet* enables it to suggest a number of things without having to articulate them directly. In both *Hamlet* and *The Lovesick King*, the crown changes hands. In *Hamlet*, it has been acquired by Claudius and is expected to pass to Hamlet, but in fact devolves on Fortinbras. In *The Lovesick King*, the crown of England is brought to Canutus after the death of Etheldred, but subsequently passes to Alured. In both cases, a Dane is the loser, and in both plays, wives are fickle, which may conceivably have expressed some unease about Anna of Denmark. More fundamentally, though, both plays suggest that crowns may be lost as well as won, and *Hamlet* explicitly declares that the Danish crown is elective, a matter of some debate among political theorists. Moreover, both plays posit an England which is subject to a foreign power, but in both cases the audience is implicitly or explicitly invited to remember that such a state of affairs was only temporary. Newcastle, so long a bulwark against the Scots, was prepared to extend only a provisional welcome to its new Scottish king, and reference to *Hamlet* helps it inject that note of caution, and to remind the audience that today's Middle Shires might yet revert to being tomorrow's northern border.

Above all, though, *The Lovesick King* is deeply invested in proclaiming Newcastle's Englishness, its wealth and its built heritage, and it implicitly argues that all are rooted in its past. It is for my purposes particularly important to note that Roger Thornton is remembered not only for supposedly building the city walls but also for his decision to 'reedifie Alhallows Church' and build a tomb for his late master there; in sharp contrast to the iconoclasm of the Reformation and the destruction wrought by the Dissolution of the Monasteries, he is a man whose sense of civic identity is rooted in the conviction that memorials and churches are important. Inhabitants of Newcastle would also have known that there was a magnificent brass memorial to Thornton himself, also in All Hallows church (although since moved to Newcastle Cathedral) with full-length images of Thornton and his wife Agnes; like St Winifred's Well it had been fortunate to survive the Reformation, but also like St Winifred's Well it testified to the continuing affection for churches, the memories they contained, and the sense of the sacred that often still inhered in them.

Notes

1 Part of this chapter is a revised version of material previously included in 'North by Northwest: Shakespeare's Shifting Frontier', in *Shakespeare in the North: Place, Politics and Performance in England and Scotland*, edited by Adam Hansen (Edinburgh UP, 2021), pp. 103–21, and in *The Edge of Christendom on the Early Modern English Stage* (De Gruyter, 2022).
2 M. Hope Dodds, '"Edmund Ironside" and "The Love-Sick King"', *The Modern Language Review* 19.2 (April, 1924), pp. 158–68, p. 164.
3 Marion Wynne-Davies, *Women Writers and Familial Discourse in the English Renaissance: Relative Values* (Basingstoke: Palgrave Macmillan, 2007), pp. 63–4.
4 Jane Lumley, *Iphigenia at Aulis, translated by Lady Lumley*, edited by Harold Hannyngton Child (Oxford: The Malone Society, 1909).
5 William, Shakespeare, *The Comedy of Errors*, edited by Stanley Wells (Harmondsworth: Penguin, 1972).
6 John Chandler, *John Leland's Itinerary: Travels in Tudor England* (Stroud: Sutton 1993), p. 340.
7 Anthony Wagner, *Heralds and Ancestors* (London: British Museum, 1978), p. 42.
8 Matthew Steggle, *Digital Humanities and the Lost Drama of Early Modern England* (Farnham: Ashgate, 2015), p. 73.
9 Todd Andrew Borlik, *Shakespeare Beyond the Green World: Drama and Ecopolitics in Jacobean Britain* (Oxford: Oxford University Press, 2023), p. 161.
10 Glyn Parry and Cathryn Enis, *Shakespeare before Shakespeare: Stratford-upon-Avon, Warwickshire, and the Elizabethan State* (Oxford: Oxford University Press, 2020), pp. 65 and 67–8.
11 Donna Hamilton, 'Catholic Use of Anglo-Saxon Precedents, 1565–1625', *Recusant History* 26.4 (October 2003): 537–55, p. 522.
12 Anthony Brewer, *The Love-Sick King, an English Tragical History with the Life and Death of Cartesmunda, the Fair Nun of Winchester* (London: Robert Pollard, 1655), sig. A2v.
13 Robert W. Dent, 'The Love-sick King: Turk Turned Dane', *The Modern Language Review* 56.4 (October 1961), pp. 555–7, p. 556.

14 Nicole Marafioti, *The King's Body: Burial and Succession in Late Anglo-Saxon England* (Toronto: University of Toronto Press, 2014), pp. 21 and 99.
15 Quoted in Eneas Mackenzie, 'Fortifications and buildings: Town walls and gates', in *Historical Account of Newcastle-Upon-Tyne Including the Borough of Gateshead* (Newcastle-upon-Tyne, 1827), pp. 105–117. Online: http://www.british-history.ac.uk/no-series/newcastle-historical-account/pp105-117.
16 J. G. A Pocock, 'Two kingdoms and three histories? Political thought in British contexts', in *Scots and Britons: Scottish Political Thought and the Union of 1603*, edited by Roger A. Mason (Cambridge: Cambridge University Press, 1994), pp. 293–312, p. 307.
17 William Shakespeare, *Macbeth*, edited by Nicholas Brooke (Oxford: Oxford University Press, 1990), 4.3.144–5.
18 William Shakespeare, *Hamlet*, edited by Harold Jenkins (London: Methuen, 1982), III.ii.172.

CODA

If some of these plays engage with *Hamlet* and *Macbeth*, then *King Lear* in turn engages with some of them. Although the supposedly historical figure of King Lear belonged to a time before the Romans, the play points at the Anglo-Saxon past in a number of respects: its use of the names Edmund, Oswald and Edgar (who apparently succeeds as King Edgar); its representation of an England being divided into different constituent realms; and its interest in female succession and in the question of whether illegitimacy was a bar to inheriting the throne, as in the apparently vexed question of Athelstan. The blinding of Gloucester might recall the use of mutilation to disqualify possible successors, as when Edward the Confessor's elder brother Alfred Aetheling was blinded by Earl Godwin, and Lear's discovery that he cannot stop rain perhaps recalls Canute's supposed failure to turn back the tide. Lost battles too were a feature of Anglo-Saxon England, both Essendon and Hastings being perceived as disastrous and era-ending. Above all, the play seems to show us a world which is both pre-Christian yet at the same time post-Catholic, since Edgar, as has often been pointed out, resembles an Elizabethan priest on the run and Kent refers to stretching on the rack, and we certainly hear the legacy of Rome in Cordelia's instruction 'a century send forth'.[1] This is a world that seems troubled by the memory of Rome in something of the same way as the great Anglo-Saxon poem *The Ruin*.

There are no sacred spaces in *King Lear*. We hear nothing of any of the places associated with the legendary King Lear such as Leicester (whose name was understood in the period as meaning Lear's castle), Bath (traditionally founded by Lear's father Bladud) or St Paul's Cathedral (on the site of which Bladud, who had made himself wings, supposedly crash-landed). To some extent, the world of the play resembles the 'topography of the holy' posited by Alexandra Walsham in which 'Protestants themselves were often compelled to seek refuge in the landscape'.[2] But it is also more simply a warning of what happens if there are no abbeys, with the bodies of Goneril and Regan carried onstage almost as if to emphasise the point that we don't know where dead royal bodies go in this society. Lear's 'You do me wrong to take me out o' th' grave' (4.7.45) may be meant metaphorically, but it also evokes a very real fear in early modern England (apparently felt by Shakespeare himself) about disturbing the dead, while his question to Cordelia, 'Where did you die?' (4.7.49) recalls anxieties about whether the road to heaven might be a literal one evidenced by debates about the orientation of burials. On the desolate heath of *King Lear*, where there are no tracks and no buildings and the only road leads over the cliff, we find the ultimate expression of the nightmare landscape feared in all these plays.

Notes

1 William Shakespeare, *King Lear*, edited by Kenneth Muir (London: Methuen, 1972), 4.4.6.
2 Alexandra Walsham, *The Reformation of the Landscape: Religion, Identity, and Memory in Early Modern Britain and Ireland* (Oxford: Oxford University Press, 2011), pp. 226 and 233.

INDEX

Adams, Max xii
Alfred the Great, King of Wessex xi, xv, 2, 41
Anna of Denmark, Queen of England 35, 46
Arden of Faversham x, 36
Ashbee, Jeremy 7
Athelstan, King of England xi, xii, xiv, xv, 2–4, 12n14, 15, 49

Boleyn, Anne 4
Borlik, Todd Andrew 10, 21, 40
Born, Hanspeter 15
Brewer, Anthony *see The Lovesick King*

Canute, King of England xi, xv, 4, 7, 8, 39, 42, 44, 49
Catherine of Valois, Queen of England xiv
Cavendish, Henry xiii
Cavendish, Sir William 27
Chapman, Alison A. xv, 35
Charles I, King of England 16
Coke, Sir Edward 16

Darby, Trudi L. 27
Dent, Robert W. 42
Di Salvo, Gina M. 35
Dissolution of the Monasteries, the x, xi, xv, 4, 47
Dodds, Hope M. 39
Drayton, Michael 1, 3
Duffy, Eamon xiv
Dunstan, Saint xiii, xv, 4, 5, 15, 17, 18, 23, 24

Eadred, King of England xi, 27
Edgar, King of England xi, xiii, xv, xvi, 15–18, 20, 21, 23, 24, 40, 49

Edethe the Empresse xiv
Edmund, King of England xi–xiii, xv, xvi, 1–4, 6, 15, 42, 49
Edmund, Saint, King of East Anglia 1, 2, 4, 10
Edward I, King of England 10, 21
Edward the Confessor, King of England 2, 4, 6, 9–11, 49
Edward the Elder, King of Wessex 2, 12n14
Edward the Martyr, King of England xiii, 16
Elden, Stuart ix
Elizabeth I, Queen of England 31, 41
Emma, Queen of England 3–8, 10
Enis, Cathryn xii, 41
Ethelred the Unready, King of England 4, 9, 16

Fludernik, Monika 30
Foot, Sarah 2, 3, 12n14
Ford, John 2
   Tis Pity She's a Whore ix
Fox, Julia xiii
Foxe, John xii, xiii, 16
Freeman, Arthur 24

Grey, Lady Jane 39, 41
Grim the Collier of Croydon 1
Guy, John xiii
Guy of Warwick xii, 3

Hamilton, Donna xii, 16, 34, 41
Hardicanute/Harthacnut, King of England xv, 4, 8
Hardwick, Bess of xiii, 27
Harold Harefoot, King of England xv, 8
Henry V, King of England xiii, xiv, 34

Henry VII, King of England xiii, 2, 36
Henry VIII, King of England 1, 5, 31
Hexham x, xii, 18–20, 23, 24
Hill, Paul 3
Hyland, Paul xiv

James I, King of England 10, 11, 35, 39, 40, 43
Jensen, Phebe 34
John a Kent and John a Cumber 16
Jones-Davies, Margaret xiv

A Knack to Know a Knave x–xii, xv–xvii, 15–25
Kocher, Paul H. 15

Leland, John 3, 40, 43
Longstaffe, Steve 24
The Lovesick King x, xv–xvii, 39–48
Lumley, John, Lord 39–41
Lumley, Lady Jane 39–41

Maclean, Sally Beth xiii, 16, 23
Manley, Lawrence xiii, 16, 23
Marafioti, Nicole xiii, 1, 6–8, 42
Marlowe, Christopher xi, xvi, 24
  Doctor Faustus xvi, 24
McCullough, Peter xvii
Middleton, Thomas
  The Lady's Tragedy ix
Mottram, Stewart xv
Munro, Lucy 1–3, 7, 9

Nora, Pierre xvi

Offa, King of Mercia xi, xv, 27, 29, 30, 32
Olaf, Saint xiv
Oswald, Saint xiii, 49

Parry, Glyn xii, 41
Persons, Robert 2, 16, 34

Ralegh, Sir Walter xiv
Rex, Peter xiii, 16, 23
Richard II of England xiii, xiv, 1
Rist, Thomas x
Ross, Peter 6

Rowley, William *see A Shoemaker a Gentleman*
Rutter, Tom 23, 24

Salvador-Bello, Mercedes 15
Savatier-Lahondès, Céline 10
Schwyzer, Philip xvi, xvii
Shakespeare, William ix, xi, xii, xiv–xvii, 10, 15, 24, 44–46, 50
  The Comedy of Errors ix
  Cymbeline xi, xiv, xv
  Hamlet xi, xiv, xvii, 33, 45, 46, 49
  Henry V ix, xi, xiv, 34
  King John ix
  King Lear 16, 49, 50
  Macbeth xi, xiv, 2, 10–12, 44, 45, 49
  Measure for Measure 6
  Romeo and Juliet xvii
  Titus Andronicus xvii
Shirley, James
  The Tragedy of St Albans 27
A Shoemaker a Gentleman x, xi, xv–xvii, 27–37, 41, 42
Steggle, Matthew 40

Thorney Abbey x, xi, xiv–xvii, 1–13, 24, 43, 44
Thornton, Roger xvi, 39, 40, 42, 43, 45, 47

Walsham, Alexandra xiii, xv, xvi, 8, 15, 30, 32, 36, 49
Warlamchester 27
Webster, John
  The Duchess of Malfi ix
The Welsh Embassador 2, 3
Westminster Abbey x, xii, xiv, xv, 1–3, 6, 7, 9–12
William the Conqueror, King of England 1
Williams, Thomas xiii, 6
Wilton Diptych 1, 10
Winchester x, xii, 2, 41, 42

Young, Francis 1, 2, 4

www.ingramcontent.com/pod-product-compliance
Lightning Source LLC
Chambersburg PA
CBHW030143170426